CREDO FOR TODAY

JOSEPH CARDINAL RATZINGER

CREDO
FOR TODAY

What Christians Believe

Translated by Michael J. Miller,
Henry Taylor, Sister Mary Frances McCarthy, Adrian Walker,
J. R. Foster, Graham Harrison, and Matthew J. O'Connell

IGNATIUS PRESS   SAN FRANCISCO

Original German edition:
Joseph Ratzinger/Benedict XVI, *Credo für heute: Was Christen glauben*
Edited by Holger Zaborowski and Alwin Letzkus
© 2006 by Libreria Editrice Vaticana, Vatican City
© 2006 by Verlag Herder, Freiburg im Breisgau

© 2009 by Ignatius Press, San Francisco
All rights reserved
ISBN-978-1-58617-247-3
Library of Congress Control Number 2008936282
Printed in the United States of America ∞

Contents

What It Means to Be a Christian

Over Everything: Love

Love is enough

A story current in late Judaism, in Jesus' time, tells how one day a pagan came to Rabbi Shammai, the famous head of a school, and told him that he would be willing to join the Jewish religion if the Rabbi could tell him about its beliefs in the time someone could stand on one leg. The Rabbi probably thought in his mind about the five books of Moses, with all the ideas in them, and everything that Jewish interpretation had added in the meantime and had declared to be equally obligatory, necessary, and essential for salvation. As he went over all this in his mind, he finally had to admit that it would be impossible for him to summarize in a couple of sentences the whole of everything that made up the religion of Israel. The strange petitioner was not a whit discouraged. He went—if we want to put it like that—to the competition: to the other famous head of a school, Rabbi Hillel, and laid the same request before him. In contrast to Rabbi Shammai, Hillel found the

Translated by Henry Taylor.

suggestion in no way impossible and answered him straight
out, "Whatever is offensive to you yourself, do not do
that to your neighbor. That is the whole law. Everything
else is interpretation." [1]

If the same man were to go today to some learned Christian theologian or other and ask him to give him, in five
minutes, a brief introduction to the essence of Christianity,
then probably all the professors would say that that was impossible: They would in any case need six semesters alone for
the basic subject of theology; and even at that, they would
scarcely have reached the edges. And yet again, it might be
possible to help the man. For the story about Rabbis Hillel
and Shammai was replayed, just a few decades after it had
first taken place, in another form. This time, a rabbi stood
before Jesus of Nazareth and asked him, "What must I do to
achieve salvation?" This is the question of what Christ himself sees as absolutely essential in his message. The Lord's
reply was this: "You shall love the Lord your God with all
your heart, and with all your soul, and with all your mind.
This is the great and first commandment. And a second is
like it, You shall love your neighbor as yourself. On these
two commandments depend all the law and the prophets"
(Mt 22:35–40). That, then, is the whole of Jesus Christ's
demand. Anyone who does this—who has love —is a Christian; he has everything (see also Rom 13:9–10).

We can see from that other passage in which Christ depicts
the Last Judgment in parabolic form that this is not meant
by Christ as just a comforting way of speaking that should
not be pushed too far; rather, it is to be understood in full
seriousness, without reservations. The Judgment represents
the real and ultimate thing; it is the test in which it is made

[1] H. Strack and P. Billerbeck, *Das Evangelium nach Matthäus, erläutert aus Talmud und Midrasch* (Munich, 1922), 357.

clear how things really stand. For here man's eternal destiny is irrevocably decided. In the parable of the Last Judgment, the Lord says that the Judge will be confronted with two kinds of men. To one group he will say, "Come, O blessed of my Father, inherit the kingdom prepared for you from the foundation of the world; for I was hungry and you gave me food, I was thirsty and you gave me drink, I was a stranger and you welcomed me, I was naked and you clothed me, I was sick and you visited me, I was in prison and you came to me." And those people will say, "When did we do all this? We have never met you." Christ will answer them, "Truly, I say to you, as you did it to one of the least of these my brethren, you did it to me." With the other group, the opposite will happen. The Judge will say to them, "Depart from me, you cursed, into the eternal fire prepared for the devil and his angels; for I was hungry and you gave me no food, I was thirsty and you gave me no drink, I was a stranger and you did not welcome me, naked and you did not clothe me, sick and in prison and you did not visit me." And these people, too, will ask, "When was all this? If we had seen you, we would have given you everything." And to them, in turn, will be said, "As you did it not to one of the least of these, you did it not to me" (Mt 25:31–46). In this parable, the Judge does not ask what kind of theory a person has held about God and the world. He is not asking about a confession of dogma, solely about love. That is enough, and it saves a man. Whoever loves is a Christian.

However great the temptation may be for theologians to quibble about this statement, to provide it with ifs and buts, notwithstanding: we may and should accept it in all its sublimity and simplicity, quite unconditionally—just as the Lord posited it. That does not mean, of course, that we should overlook the fact that these words represent a not inconsiderable proposition and make no small demand on someone.

For love, as it is here portrayed as the content of being a
Christian, demands that we try to live as God lives. He loves
us, not because we are especially good, particularly virtu-
ous, or of any great merit, not because we are useful or even
necessary to him; he loves us, not because *we* are good, but
because *he* is good. He loves us, although we have nothing
to offer him; he loves us even in the ragged raiment of the
prodigal son, who is no longer wearing anything lovable. To
love in the Christian sense means trying to follow in this
path: not just loving someone we like, who pleases us, who
suits us, and certainly not just someone who has something
to offer us or from whom we are hoping to gain some
advantage.

Practicing Christian love in the same way as Christ means
that we are good to someone who needs our kindness, even
if we do not like him. It means committing ourselves to
the way of Jesus Christ and thus bringing about something
like a Copernican revolution in our own lives. For in a
certain sense, we are all still living before Copernicus, so to
speak. Not only in that we think, to all appearances, that
the sun rises and sets and goes around the earth, but in a
far more profound sense. For we all carry within us that
inborn illusion by virtue of which each of us takes his own
self to be the center of things, around which the world and
everyone else have to turn. We all necessarily find ourselves, time and again, construing and seeing other things
and people solely in relation to our own selves, regarding
them as satellites, as it were, revolving around the hub of
our own self. Becoming a Christian, according to what we
have just said, is something quite simple and yet completely
revolutionary. It is just this: achieving the Copernican revolution and no longer seeing ourselves as the center of the
universe, around which everyone else must turn, because
instead of that we have begun to accept quite seriously that

we are one of many among God's creatures, all of whom turn around God as their center.

Why do we need faith?

Being a Christian means having love. That is unbelievably difficult and, at the same time, incredibly simple. Yet however difficult it may be in many respects, discovering this is still a profoundly liberating experience. You will probably say, however: Well and good, that is what Jesus' message is about, and that is very fine and comforting. But what have you theologians and priests made of it, what has the Church made of it? If love is enough, why do we have your dogma? Why do we have faith, which is forever competing with science? Is it not really true, then, what liberal scholars have said, that Christianity has been corrupted by the fact that, instead of talking with Christ about God the Father and being like brothers to each other, people have constructed a doctrine of Christ; by the fact that people, instead of leading others to mutual service, have invented an intolerant dogma; by the fact that instead of urging people to love, they have demanded belief and made being a Christian depend on a confession of faith?

There is no doubt that there is something terribly serious in this question, and like all really weighty questions, it cannot be dealt with just like that, with a well-turned phrase. At the same time, however, we cannot miss the fact that it also involves a simplification. To see this clearly, we need only realistically apply our reflections so far to our own lives. Being a Christian means having love; it means achieving the Copernican revolution in our existence, by which we cease to make ourselves the center of the universe, with everyone else revolving around us.

If we look at ourselves honestly and seriously, then there is not just something liberating in this marvelously simple message. There is also something most disturbing. For who among us can say he has never passed by anyone who was hungry or thirsty or who needed us in any way? Who among us can say that he truly, in all simplicity, carries out the service of being kind to others? Who among us would not have to admit that even in the acts of kindness he practices toward others, there is still an element of selfishness, something of self-satisfaction and looking back at ourselves? Who among us would not have to admit that he is more or less living in the pre-Copernican illusion and looking at other people, seeing them as real only in their relationship to our own selves? Thus, the sublime and liberating message of love, as being the sole and sufficient content of Christianity, can also become something very demanding.

It is at this point that faith begins. For what faith basically means is just that this shortfall that we all have in our love is made up by the surplus of Jesus Christ's love, acting on our behalf. He simply tells us that God himself has poured out among us a superabundance of his love and has thus made good in advance all our deficiency. Ultimately, faith means nothing other than admitting that we have this kind of shortfall; it means opening our hand and accepting a gift. In its simplest and innermost form, faith is nothing but reaching that point in love at which we recognize that we, too, need to be given something. Faith is thus that stage in love which really distinguishes it as love; it consists in overcoming the complacency and self-satisfaction of the person who says, "I have done everything, I don't need any further help." It is only in "faith" like this that selfishness, the real opposite of love, comes to an end. To that extent, faith is already present in and with true loving; it simply represents that impulse in love which leads to its finding its true self: the openness of someone who does not insist on his own capabilities, but is aware of receiving something as a gift and of standing in need of it.

This faith is of course susceptible to many and varied developments and interpretations. We need only to become aware that the gesture of opening our hand, of being able to receive in all simplicity, through which love first attains its inner purity, is grasping at nothing unless there is someone who can fill our hands with the grace of forgiveness. And thus once again everything would have to end in idle waste, in meaninglessness, if the answer to this, namely, Christ, did not exist. Thus, true loving necessarily passes into the gesture of faith, and in that gesture lies a demand for the mystery of Christ, a reaching out toward it—and that mystery, when it unfolds, is a necessary development of that basic gesture; to reject it would be to reject both faith and love.

And yet, conversely, however true this may be—and however much christological and ecclesiastical faith is for that reason absolutely necessary—at the same time, it remains true that everything we encounter in dogma is, ultimately, just interpretation: interpretation of the one truly sufficient and decisive fundamental reality of the love between God and men. And it remains true, consequently, that those people who are truly loving, who are as such also believers, may be called Christians.

The law of superabundance

Starting from this basic understanding of Christianity, Scripture and dogma can be read and understood in a new way. I will mention only a couple of examples, passages from Holy Scripture that at first seem quite inaccessible to us and then, all at once, in this light, open up for us. Let us recall, for instance, the saying in the Sermon on the Mount that we met the day before yesterday in all its awesomeness: "You have heard that it was said to the men of old, 'You shall not kill; and whoever kills shall be liable to the judgment.' But I say to you that every one who is angry with his brother shall be liable to judgment; whoever insults his brother shall be liable to the council, and whoever says 'You fool!' shall be liable to the hell of fire" (Mt 5:21–22). Whenever we read this passage, it weighs on us; it crushes us. Yet there is a verse just before that gives the passage its whole meaning when it says, "I tell you, unless your righteousness exceeds that of the scribes and Pharisees, you will never enter the kingdom of heaven" (Mt 5:20). The key word in this verse is "exceeds". The original Greek is still more strongly expressed, and only that really shows the basic intention here. In literal translation, it says, "Unless your righteousness has more superabundance than that of the scribes and Pharisees. . . ."

Here we meet with a theme that runs through the whole of Christ's message. The Christian is the person who does not calculate; rather, he does something extra. He is in fact the lover, who does not ask, "How much farther can I go and still remain within the realm of venial sin, stopping short of mortal sin?" Rather, the Christian is the one who simply seeks what is good, without any calculation. A merely righteous man, the one who is only concerned with doing what is correct, is a Pharisee; only he who is not merely righteous is beginning to be a Christian. Of course, that does not, by a long way, mean that a Christian is a person who does nothing wrong and has no failings. On the contrary, he is the person who knows that he does have failings and who is generous with God and with other people because he knows how much he depends on the generosity of God and of his fellowmen. The generosity of someone who knows he is in debt to everyone else, who is quite unable to attempt to maintain a correctness that would allow him to make strict demands in return: that is the true guiding light of the ethical code that Jesus is proclaiming (cf. Mt 18:13–35). This is the mystery, at once incredibly demanding and liberating, to be found behind the word "superabundance", without which there can be no Christian righteousness.

If we look closer, we realize at once that the basic relationship we have discovered through the idea of "superabundance" is characteristic of the whole story of God's dealings with man, indeed, that it is, moreover, as it were, the characteristic trait of divinity in creation itself. The miracle at Cana and the miracle of feeding the five thousand are signs of that superabundance of generosity which is essential to God's way of acting, that way of doing things which in the process of creation squanders millions of seeds so as to save *one* living one. That way of doing things which lavishly produces an entire universe in order to prepare a place on earth for that mysterious being, man. That way of doing things by which, in a final, unheard-of lavishness, he gives himself away in order to save that "thinking reed", man, and to bring him to his goal. This ultimate and unheard-of event will always defy the calculating minds of correct thinkers. It can really be understood only on the basis of the foolishness of a love that discards any notion of calculation and is unafraid of any lavishness. And yet, again, it is no more than the logical conclusion of that lavishness which is, as it were, on all sides the personal stamp of the Creator and is now likewise set to become the basic rule for our own existence before God and men.

Let us go back to what we were saying. We said that, on the basis of this perception (which, in turn, is only an application of the principle of "love"), not only do the patterns of creation and of salvation history become comprehensible, but also the meaning of the demands Jesus makes on us, as we meet them in the Sermon on the Mount. It is certainly most helpful to know from the start that they are not to be understood in a legalistic sense. Teachings like this: "If any one strikes you on the right cheek, turn to him the other also; and if anyone ... take your coat, let him have your cloak as well" (Mt 5:39f.) are not articles of law that we have to carry out as particular commands in a literal sense. They are not articles, but vivid examples and images, which, taken together, are intended to give direction. And yet that is not enough to arrive at a real understanding of them. We have to dig deeper for that and to see that in the Sermon on the Mount, on one hand, a merely moralistic interpretation—which understands everything that is said as commandments, so that if we do not keep them we will go to hell—is inadequate: seen like that, it would not raise us up but crush us. Yet, on the other hand, an interpretation merely in terms of grace is likewise inadequate, an interpretation asserting that all that is being shown here is how worthless all our human actions and activity are; that this merely makes clear that we can achieve nothing and that all is grace. Such an interpretation says that this passage is just making it clear that in the night of human sinfulness all distinctions are trivial and that no one has any rights he can insist on, anyway, because everyone deserves damnation and everyone is saved only by grace. Certainly, this passage makes us conscious, with appalling clarity, of our need for forgiveness; it shows how little reason any man has for boasting and for setting himself apart from sinners as a righteous man. But the point of it is something different. It is not just intended to set us all against a background of judgment and forgiveness, which would then make all human activity a matter of indifference. It has another aim as well, which is to give directions for our life: it is intended to point us toward that "extra", that "superabundance" and generosity, which does not mean that we suddenly become faultless and "perfect" people, but it does mean that we try to adopt the attitude of the lover, who does not calculate but simply—loves.

And finally, the quite concrete christological backdrop of the Sermon on the Mount is part of this. The call for something "more" does not simply ring out from the unapproachable and eternal majesty of God; rather, it sounds forth from the mouth of the Lord, in whom God has given away his own self into the wretchedness of human history. God himself lives and works according to the rule of superabundance, of that love which can give nothing less than itself. That is the simple answer to the question about the essence of Christianity, which confronts us again at the end and which, properly understood, includes everything.

Faith, hope, and love

There is still one thing for us to think about at the end. Through talking about love, we came upon faith. We saw that, properly understood, faith is present within love and that only faith can bring love to its proper end, because our own loving would remain just as inadequate as an open hand stretched out into emptiness. If we think a little further, we also come upon the mystery of hope. For our believing and our loving are still on their way, so long as we remain in this world, and again and again they are in danger of flickering out. It is truly Advent. No one can say of himself, "I *am* completely saved." In the era of this world, there is no redemption as a past action, already completed; nor does it exist as a complete and final present reality; redemption exists only in the mode of hope. The light of

God does not shine in this world except in the lamps of hope that his loving-kindness has set up on our way. How often that distresses us: we would like more; we would like the whole thing, round, unassailably present. Yet basically we have to say: Could there be any more human way of redeeming us than that which declares us to be beings in the course of development, on our way, that tells us we may hope? Could there be a better light for us, as nomadic beings, than the one that sets us free to go forward without fear, because we know that the light of eternal love stands at the end of the road?

Tomorrow, Wednesday, an Advent Ember Day, we shall encounter this very mystery of hope in the liturgy of the Holy Mass. The Church sets it before us on this particular day in the shape of the Mother of the Lord, the Blessed Virgin Mary. For these weeks of Advent she stands before us as the woman who is carrying the Hope of the world just under her heart and, thus, going before us on our way as a symbol of hope. She stands there as the woman in whom what is humanly impossible has become possible, through God's saving mercy. And thus she becomes a symbol for us all. For if it is up to us, if it depends on the feeble flame of our goodwill and the paltry sum of our actions, we cannot achieve salvation. However much we are capable of, it is not enough for that. It remains impossible. Yet God, in his mercy, has made the impossible possible. We need only say, in all humility, "Behold, I am a servant of the Lord" (cf. Lk 2:37f.; Mk 10:27). Amen.

God

"I Believe in One God, the Father Almighty"

What does it really mean when a person decides to believe in God, the Father Almighty, maker of heaven and earth? The content of such a decision will, perhaps, be best understood if we look first at two current misunderstandings that fail to take into account the essential meaning of such a faith. The first misunderstanding consists in regarding the question of God as a purely theoretical one that, in the last analysis, has no impact on the course of the world or of one's own life. According to positivistic philosophy, it is impossible to prove such propositions either true or false; that is, there is no possibility of showing clearly that they are false, but this very fact testifies to their lack of importance. For if something that is, to all intents and purposes, unprovable as true can also not be rejected as false, it is clear that nothing in man's life will be altered by it whether it is true or false; it can, therefore, be comfortably ignored.[1] Theoretical irrefutability becomes thus a sign of practical

Translated by Sister Mary Frances McCarthy, S.N.D.

[1] On the subject of positivism, cf. Bernhard Casper, "Die Unfähigkeit zur Gottesfrage im positivistischen Bewusstsein", in *Die Frage nach Gott*, ed. Joseph Ratzinger, 27–42 (Freiburg: Herder, 1972); Norbert Schiffers, "Die Welt als

negligibility; what has no impact has also no meaning. Anyone who is aware of the contradictory situations in which Christianity is involved today, of how, by reason of its monarchical and nationalistic structures, it has come to be regarded as an appurtenance of Marxist thought, might indeed be tempted to consider the faith of Christians as a useless placebo that can be used as one will because it has no content of its own.

But there also exists a diametrically opposed view. Its proponents maintain that belief in God is but the expedient of a particular social group, in terms of which it can be fully explained and with the disappearance of which it, too, will disappear. It was invented to ensure domination and to keep man subservient to existing powers. And if there are some who see in the God of Israel a revolutionary principle, they, too, are basically in accord with this view: they are merely equating the notion of God with the praxis that seems right to them.

One who reads the Bible will have no doubt as to the practical character of the profession of faith in God, the Almighty. The Bible makes it abundantly clear that a world under God's sway is quite different from a world without God—that nothing, in fact, remains the same if God is taken away and that, by the same token, everything changes when one turns to God. Husbands, for instance, are told almost, as it were, parenthetically, in Paul's first epistle to the Thessalonians (4:3–5), that their relationship to their wives is to be marked by a holy respect, "not giving way to selfish lust like the pagans who do not know God". The change that takes place when God enters the context of human life reaches to the most personal and intimate level of human

Tatsache", in *Gott-Mensch-Universum*, ed. Johannes Hüttenbügel, 31–69 (Gras: Styria, 1974).

relationships; ignorance of God, atheism, finds its concrete expression in a lack of respect for one's fellowmen, whereas knowledge of God means seeing them in a new way.

This same fact is affirmed in the other texts in which Paul speaks of atheism. In the epistle to the Galatians (4:8–9), he designates as the characteristic effect of ignorance of God enslavement to the "elemental principles of this world", with which one enters into a kind of worshipful relationship that soon turns to slavery because it rests on untruth; the Christian can ridicule these elemental principles as "pitiable" and "despicable" because he knows the truth and is thereby free of their tyranny. In the epistle to the Romans (1:18–32), Paul develops this thought further. In speaking of the philosophy of the heathens and its relationship to existing religions, he notes that the Mediterranean nations have reduced the knowledge of God to mere theory and, by reason of this perversion, have themselves fallen into perversity; by excluding from their way of life the foundation of all things, whom they very well know, they have distorted reality and have become disoriented, without norms and incapable of distinguishing what is base from what is noble, what is great from what is ordinary, and are thus, in practice, susceptible to every perversity—a train of thought to which we cannot deny a certain validity for the present as well.

If we turn our attention, finally, to the central Old Testament text about belief in God, it, too, affirms what has been said. In it, the revelation of God's name (Ex 3) is, at the same time, the revelation of God's will; it changes everything not only in the life of Moses but also in the lives of the people and, hence, in the history of the world. Significantly, it is not a concept of God that is propounded here but a name that is revealed. We are offered, not a series of theological deliberations leading to a certain conclusion, but a relationship that is comparable to the relationship between persons, yet superior to it because it alters the foundation of life itself, or, more accurately, it exposes to the light the foundation of life that has hitherto been hidden and turns it into a summons, a call. That is why the Israelite regards the daily repetition of the act by which he professes his belief in God as the acceptance of the yoke of God's dominion; praying the credo is the act by which he lays claim to his place in reality.

One more fact must be noted here—a fact that is assuredly most repugnant to a mind that would remain neutral. My thought is well expressed in the above-mentioned passage from the epistle to the Galatians in which Paul, having recalled the atheistic past of those to whom he is writing, adds the comment: But now you have acknowledged God— and immediately corrects himself: or rather, you have been acknowledged by God (Gal 4:9). A universal experience finds expression here: knowing and believing in God is an active-passive process, not a philosophical structure, whether theoretical or practical; it is an act in which one is first touched by God and then responds in thought and deed but which one is, however, free to reject. It is only from this perspective that we can understand what it means to call God a "Person" or to speak of "revelation": in our knowledge of God there occurs also—and, indeed, first— something from God's side. God is not a resting object but the ground of our being, who establishes his own credentials, who makes his presence known at the very center of our being, and who can, precisely for this reason, be ignored because we are so easily inclined to live far from the center of our being, far from ourselves. By revealing the passive element in our knowledge of God, we have also touched the roots of the two misunderstandings of which we spoke at the beginning. Both of them presume a knowledge in which the individual is himself active. They know man only as an active subject in the world and see the whole of reality as but a system of lifeless objects manipulated by man. It is precisely at this point, however, that faith offers a different perspective. Only here can we begin to understand what faith really is.

But let us not move too quickly. Before going on, let us first review what has already been said. We have seen that the sentence "I believe in God, the Father Almighty" is not just a theoretical formula with no implications of further meaning. Its validity or lack of validity alters the very foundations of the world. The next step is to turn our attention to Werner Heisenberg's formulation of this thought in his conversations about science and religion. His account of what the physicist Wolfgang Pauli said to him in 1927 has an unmistakably prophetic ring. Pauli was afraid that the collapse of religious convictions would be followed all too shortly by the collapse of the existing ethical code, ". . . and there will happen things so terrible that we cannot even conceive of them now." [2] At the time, no one could have known how soon thereafter mockery of the God of Jesus Christ as a Jewish invention would turn into fact what had hitherto been unthinkable.

In the same discussion, Heisenberg attacked with great energy the question that has thus far gone unanswered in our deliberations: Is it perhaps correct to say that "God" is merely the function of a particular praxis? Heisenberg reports that he asked the great Danish physicist Niels Bohr if God

---

[2] Werner Heisenberg, *Der Teil und das Ganze: Gespräche im Umkreis der Atomphysik* (Munich: Piper, 1969), 118. A comment from the year 1952 reechoes this thought: "Once the magnetic force that guides this compass has been completely eliminated, . . . I am afraid very terrible things will happen—worse things even than concentration camps and atom bombs" (195). [For an English translation of this work, see Werner Heisenberg, *Physics and Beyond: Encounters and Conversations*, trans. Arnold J. Pomerans (New York: Harper & Row, 1971).]

should not be relegated to the same level of reality as certain imaginary numbers in the field of mathematics that do not exist as natural numbers but on which whole branches of mathematics have been built, so that "there are such numbers, after all. . . . Would it not be possible in religion, too, . . . to regard the expression 'there is' as the ascent to a higher level of abstraction? This ascent would have the function of facilitating our understanding of cosmic connections, nothing more." [3] Is God a kind of moral fiction in terms of which it is possible to present spiritual contexts in an abstract and synoptical way? That is the question that is raised here.

In the same conversation, Heisenberg approaches another aspect of the problem—the concept of religion proposed by Max Planck. On the model of nineteenth-century thought, this great scholar differentiated strictly between the objective and subjective aspects of the world. The objective aspect can be investigated with exact scientific procedures; but the subjective aspect rests on personal decisions that are beyond the categories of true and false. To these subjective decisions, which each must make for himself alone, he assigned the realm of religion, which can therefore be lived with personal conviction without impinging on the objective world of science. Heisenberg reports that it became clear to him during a conversation with Wolfgang Pauli that such a total rift between knowing and believing would "hardly be more than an emergency measure adopted for a limited period of time". [4] To separate religion, belief in God, from objective truth is to fail to recognize its innermost nature. "Religion is concerned with objective truth." This, says Heisenberg, was Niels Bohr's answer to the question.

---

[3] Heisenberg, *Der Teil und das Ganze*, 126.
[4] Ibid., 117–18.

Heisenberg added: "But it seems to me that the whole division into objective and subjective aspects of the world is carried too far here." [5]

It is not necessary for our purpose to examine how Bohr, in his conversation with Heisenberg, overemphasized the scientific aspect of the distinction between objective and subjective and searched for a central order behind the two. Even without this, the point at issue is clear: belief in God does not claim to offer a fictitious and abstract union of different modes of action; it claims to be more than a subjective conviction inexplicably juxtaposed to a godless objectivity. It claims to reveal the essence, the root, of the objective, to bring into sharper focus the demands of objective reality. It does so by leading to that source which unites object and subject and offers the only true explanation of their relationship. Einstein pointed out that the relationship of subject and object is, ultimately, the greatest of all puzzles, or, more exactly, that our thinking, our mathematical worlds conceived solely in our consciousness, correspond to reality, that our consciousness has the same structure as reality and vice versa. [6] That is the principal ground on which all science rests. It acts as though this were a matter of course, whereas, in fact, nothing is less so. For it means that all being has the same nature as consciousness; that there is present in human thought, in human subjectivity, that which objectively moves the world. The world itself has the same nature as consciousness. The subjective is not something alien to objective reality; rather, this reality is itself like a subject. The subjective is objective, and vice versa. This affects even the language of natural science, which here,

[5] Ibid., 123ff.; 126–30.

[6] Quoted here from Josef Pieper, "Kreatürlichkeit: Bemerkungen über die Elemente eines Grundbegriffs", in *Thomas von Aquin 1274–1974*, ed. Ludger Oeing-Hanhoff, 47–70 (Munich: Kösel, 1974). Quotation is on 50.

under the pressure of objects, often reveals more than its users are aware.

An example from an entirely different sphere suggests itself: even the most obstinate neo-Darwinists, who want to exclude from evolution every final, goal-directed cause so as not to be suspected of metaphysics or of belief in God, nevertheless speak with total artlessness of how nature contrives to profit by the best chances of survival. One who studies their customary linguistic usage cannot fail to conclude that nature is here consistently endowed with the attributes of God, or, more exactly perhaps: it has appropriated the very place ascribed in the Old Testament to wisdom. It is a conscious power acting with utmost intelligence. Without doubt, these scientists would explain, if asked, that the word nature is here only an abstract schematization of many individual elements—somewhat in the nature of an imaginary number that serves to facilitate the construction of theories and make them more comprehensible. But we must seriously ask ourselves whether any part of this whole theory would survive were we strictly to prohibit this latter fiction and insist on its elimination. We know for a fact that no logical context would remain.

Josef Pieper has shed light on our subject from yet another perspective. He reminds us that, according to Sartre, human beings and things cannot have a nature. If they did, Sartre argues, there would have to be a God. If reality itself does not proceed from a creative consciousness, if it is not the realization of a design, of an idea, then it will always be a structure without firm contours, to be used as one will; but if there are meaningful forms in it that are antecedent to man, then there must also be a meaning that is responsible for their existence. For Sartre, the one unchanging certainty was that there is no God; therefore, there can be no nature. This means that man is condemned to a monstrous freedom; he must discover for himself with no norm to guide him what he will make of himself and of the world.[7] At this point, the nature of the alternative with which we are confronted in the first article of the Creed should be growing gradually clear. The question is whether we accept reality as pure matter or as the expression of a meaning that refers to us; whether we invent values or must find them. On our answer depends the kind of freedom of which we must speak, for two completely different freedoms, two completely different fundamental attitudes toward life, are involved here.

Many, perhaps, will feel compelled to object to these considerations on the grounds that what has been said thus far is just fruitless speculation about the God of the philosophers; it has no relevance to the living God of Abraham, Isaac, and Jacob, the Father of Jesus Christ. The Bible, they will protest, does not speak about a central order (as Heisenberg does)[8] or about nature and being (as the early philosophers did); to do so would be to dilute faith, which is concerned with the Father, with Jesus Christ, with I and thou, with a personal relationship with the living God through prayer. Such objections may sound pious, but they miss the point and conceal the greatness of the real object of faith. Granted, God cannot be measured as we might measure some measurable object. Granted, too, there is no measuring without the intellectual context that links the measurer with the measured. But, for that very reason, this foundation cannot itself be measured; it is antecedent to all measuring. Greek philosophy expressed the thought in this

[7] Pieper has referred repeatedly and with increasing emphasis to this question, most recently in the above-mentioned publication, esp. 50.

[8] Heisenberg, *Der Teil und das Ganze*, 118. The central concept is the one contained in the second conversation ("Positivism, Metaphysics, and Religion") (1952), 291ff.

way: The ultimate foundations of all proof, on which thought rests, are never measured; they are only perceived. But everyone knows that perception is something unique. It is not to be separated from the intellectual stance an individual has adopted during his lifetime. The deepest perceptions of man require the whole man. It is clear, then, that such knowledge has its own mode of existence. We cannot verify God as we would verify some measurable object. There is question here also of an act of humility; the acceptance of the fact that one's own intellect has been called by the eternal intellect. Counter to this is the desire for an autonomy that first invents the world and then opposes to the Christian humility of acknowledgment of being that other strange humility which despises being: in himself, man is nothing, an unfinished animal, but perhaps we can still make something of him . . .

If we distinguish too closely between the God of faith and the God of the philosophers, we deprive faith of its objectivity and again split object and subject into two different worlds. Granted, there can be many different approaches to the one God. Heisenberg's conversations with friends show how a mind that is sincerely seeking can penetrate through the spirit in nature to a central order that not only exists but makes demands upon us and, by its demands, becomes present to us, becomes like the soul: the central order can be present to us just as the center of a human being can be present to another human being. It can meet us.[9] For one who has grown up in the Christian tradition, the way begins in the "thou" of prayer: such a one knows that he can address the Lord; that this Jesus is not just a historical personage of the past but is the same in all ages. And he knows, too, that in, with, and through the Lord he can address him to whom

[9] Ibid., 293.

Jesus says "Father". In Jesus, he sees, likewise, the Father.
For he sees that this Jesus does not have his life from himself,
that his whole existence is an exchange with the Other, a
coming from him and a returning to him. He sees that this
Jesus is truly "Son" in his whole existence, is one who receives
his inmost being from another, that his life is a receiving. In
him is to be found the hidden foundation; in the actions,
words, life, suffering of him who is truly Son it is possible to
see, hear, and touch him who is unknown. The unknown
ground of being reveals itself as Father.[10] Omnipotence is
like a father. God no longer appears as Supreme Being in
the process of becoming, or as Being per se, but as Person.
And yet: the personal relationship that exists here is not to
be equated with purely human relationships—to that extent,
it is an oversimplification to speak of our relationship with
God in terms of an I-thou relationship. Speaking to God
does not mean speaking with just anyone who happens to
stand before me as another "thou"; on the contrary, it touches
the ground of my own being, without which I would not
be, and this ground of my being is identical with the ground
of being per se; indeed, it is that being without which nothing is. What is so striking here is, of course, the fact that this
whole ground of being is, at the same time, a relationship;
not less than I, who know, think, feel, and love, but rather
more than I, so that I can know only because I am known,
love only because I am already loved. The first article of the
Creed signifies, then, a highly personal and, at the same time,
a highly objective knowledge. A highly personal knowledge:

[10] This thought is developed at greater length in my essay "Anthropological Foundation of the Concept of Tradition", in *Principles of Catholic Theology: Building Stones for a Fundamental Theology*, trans. Sister Mary Frances
McCarthy, S.N.D. (San Francisco: Ignatius Press, 1987), 85–101. On what
follows, see my *Introduction to Christianity*, trans. J. R. Foster, rev. ed. (San
Francisco: Ignatius Press, 2004), 52–57.

the finding of a "thou" who gives me meaning, to whom I can entrust myself absolutely. That is why this first article is formulated, not as a neutral sentence, but as a prayer, an address: I believe in God—I believe in thee, I entrust myself to thee. Where God is truly known, he is not something we can discuss as we would discuss imaginary or natural numbers, but a "thou" to whom we can speak because he speaks to us. I can entrust myself absolutely to him because he is absolute, because his person is the objective ground of all reality. Confidence and trust as firmly based realities are possible in this world only because the ground of being is trustworthy—if this were not so, all the trust of individuals would be, in the last analysis, but an empty farce or a tragic irony.

Is it necessary, after these reflections, to turn again to the questions raised at the beginning, in which there lurks the objection so frequently raised by Marxism today—that God is but the imaginary number by which the ruling class makes its power visible; that a view of life contained in the concepts "Father" and "omnipotence" and requiring worship of this Father and this omnipotence is revealed to be a credo of oppression; that only the radical emancipation of Father and omnipotence can restore freedom? To do so, we would have to retrace our whole train of thought from this one perspective; but perhaps, after all that has been said, it will suffice if, instead, I recall a scene from Solzhenitsyn's *August 1914* that has a direct bearing on these questions. In the extraordinary circumstances created by the patriotic upsurge at the beginning of the war in 1914, two Russian students, enthusiastic as are nearly all their generation about revolutionary social ideas, engage in conversation with an unusual wise man to whom they have given the nickname "the astrologist". He attempts very cautiously to woo them from the specter of a scientifically conceived social order and to show them how illusory is the hope that the world can be changed by a revolutionary intellect: "Who would be so presumptuous as to claim he has the ability to *invent* ideal conditions? ... Presumption is the mark of limited intellectual development. A person whose intellectual development is limited is presumptuous; one whose intellect is highly developed is humble." In the end, after much back and forth, the young men ask: "But isn't justice a sufficient principle on which to found a social order?" And the answer: "By all means! But not our own justice as we imagine it for ourselves in some comfortable earthly paradise. Rather, that justice that is before us, that exists without us and for its own sake. And we must *conform* to it."[11] Solzhenitsyn has been at pains to stress the antithetical concepts invent/ conform in various ways in the printed text: "invent" in boastful capitals, "conform" in humble italics. Nevertheless, the key issue is not "invent" but "conform". Without mentioning the word God, and with the hesitancy of one who must lead to the center those who have gone far astray ("... he spoke; he looked at both of them; had he not perhaps gone too far?"), the author describes very precisely what worship is, what the first article of the Creed is all about. For man, the key issue is not invention but conformity, attention to the justice of the Creator, to the truth of creation itself. That is the only guarantee of freedom; it alone ensures that inviolable respect of person for person, for God's creature, which, according to Paul, is the mark of one who knows God. Conformity of this kind, acceptance of the truth of the Creator in his creatures, is worship. That is what is at issue when we say: I believe in one God, the Father Almighty, maker of heaven and earth.

[11] Aleksandr Solzhenitsyn, *August 1914*, trans. Michael Glenny (New York: Farrar, Straus and Giroux, 1972), 409 and 412. See also all of chap. 42, 395–412.

Creation

Belief in Creation and the Theory of Evolution

In the mid-nineteenth century, when Charles Darwin developed the idea of the evolution of all living things and thus radically called into question the traditional notion of the invariability of the species created by God, he inaugurated a revolution in our world view that was no less thoroughgoing than the one that we associate with the name Copernicus. Despite the Copernican revolution, which dethroned the earth and increasingly expanded the dimensions of the universe toward the infinite, as a whole the firmly established framework of the old world view continued to exist and to insist, without modification, on the temporal boundary of the six thousand years that had been calculated from the biblical chronologies. A few examples may illustrate for us the tenacity (almost unimaginable today) with which people used to take for granted the narrow temporal parameters of the biblical world view.

In 1848, when Jacob Grimm published his *History of the German Language*, he regarded the age of mankind—six thousand years—as an undisputed postulate that needed no further

Translated by Michael J. Miller.

reflection. W. Wachsmuth declared the same thing as a matter of course in his widely acclaimed *General History of Culture*, which appeared in 1850 and in this respect was no different from the general history of the world and of peoples that Christian Daniel Beck had published in its second edition in 1813. The examples could easily be multiplied.[1] Let these suffice to indicate the narrow horizon within which our view of history and of the world still ranged a hundred years ago and to show how unshakable was the Bible-based tradition of thought taken entirely from Judeo-Christian salvation history; what a revolution it must have been, after the immeasurable expansion of space that had preceded it, for a similar abolition of boundaries to take control now of time and history! In many respects the consequences of such a process are even more dramatic than those of the Copernican revolution could ever be. For the dimension of time touches the creature man incomparably more deeply than that of space; indeed, now the notion of space, too, is once again relativized and changed, inasmuch as space loses its firm, definable form and is itself subjected to history, to temporality. Man appears as the being that came to be in and through endless changes; the great constants of the biblical world view, the original condition and the final condition, become unfathomably remote—the basic understanding of reality changes: becoming replaces being, evolution replaces creation, and ascent replaces the Fall.

Within the context of these reflections we cannot thoroughly investigate the host of questions that are posed thereby; we merely wish to state the problem of whether the fundamental world views of creation and evolution can

---

[1] This material is taken from J. Dörmann, "War Johann Jakob Bachofen Evolutionist?" *Anthropos* 60 (1965): 1–48; specifically, 23ff.

(contrary to first impressions) coexist without forcing the theologian to make a dishonest compromise and for tactical reasons to declare the terrain that has become untenable as superfluous anyway, after having so short a time before insisted loudly on situating it as an indispensable part of the faith.

The problem has various levels, which we must distinguish from each other and evaluate separately. First, there is a relatively superficial aspect of the whole matter, which is really not entirely theological: the pre-Darwinian idea of the invariability of the species had been justified in terms of the idea of creation; it regarded every individual species as a datum of creation that had existed since the beginning of the world through God's creative work as something unique and different alongside the other species. It is clear that this form of belief in creation contradicts the idea of evolution and that this expression of the faith has become untenable today. But with this correction (and we will return again later to examine its significance and problematic character), we have not exhausted the entire scope of the concept of creation. When one rules out all individual creations and replaces them with the idea of evolution, then the real difference between the two concepts first emerges; it becomes clear that each one is based on a different way of thinking, a different intellectual approach, and a different way of framing the question. The extension of the concept of creation into the individual structures of reality was of course able for a long time to conceal this deeper difference and thus the real problem. Belief in creation inquires into the fact that there is being as such; its question is why anything exists at all instead of nothing. In contrast, the idea of evolution asks why precisely these things exist and not others, whence they acquired their particularity, and how they are connected with other formations.[2] Philosophically, then, one would say that the idea of evolution is situated on the phenomenological level and deals with the actually occurring individual forms in the world, whereas the belief in creation moves on the ontological level, inquires into what is behind individual things, marvels at the miracle of being itself, and tries to give an account of the puzzling "is" that we commonly predicate of all existing realities. One could also put it this way: Belief in creation concerns the difference between nothing and something, while the idea of evolution examines the difference between something and something else. Creation characterizes being as a whole as "being from somewhere else." Evolution, in contrast, describes the inner structure of being and inquires into the specific "from where" of individual existing realities. Perhaps for the natural scientist the problem as framed by belief in creation appears to be an illegitimate question that man cannot answer. The transition to the evolutionary way of looking at the world is in fact the step toward that positivistic form of science that deliberately restricts itself to what is given, tangible, and empirically observable by man, thereby rejecting from the realm of science as unproductive any reflection about the real foundations of reality. In this regard, belief in creation and the idea of evolution designate not only two different areas of inquiry but also two different categories of thought. That is probably the cause of the problematic relation that one senses between the two even after their fundamental compatibility has become evident.

But this leads us already to a second level of the question. We have learned to distinguish two aspects of belief in creation: its concrete expression in the notion of the creation of all the individual species by God and its real

[2] Cf. H. Volk, *Schöpfungsglaube und Entwicklung* (Münster, 1955).

intellectual starting point. We have established that the first
aspect, that is, the concrete form which the idea of creation had taken in practice, has been abolished by the idea
of evolution; here the believer must allow himself to be
taught by science that the way in which he had imagined
creation was part of a pre-scientific world view that has
become untenable. But as far as the actual intellectual
approach is concerned, the inquiry into the transition from
nothingness to being, we have managed for the time being
to note only the difference between the two categories of
thought; the theory of evolution and belief in creation
belong, with respect to their ultimate fundamental orientation, to entirely different intellectual worlds and have nothing at all directly in common. Meanwhile what are we to
think about this apparent neutrality that we have thus stumbled upon? That is the second level of the inquiry, which
we must now pursue further. Here it is not very easy to
make progress, because there is always something very delicate about comparing categories of thought and about the
problem of whether they can be related to each other. In
doing so one must try to position oneself *above* both categories of thought and thus easily ends up in an intellectual no-man's land, in which one appears suspicious to both
sides and soon gets the feeling of straddling the fence. Nevertheless, we must make the attempt to grope our way
farther. As an initial observation, we can state that the inquiry
of evolutionary thought is narrower than that of belief
in creation. By no means, therefore, can evolutionary doctrine incorporate belief in creation. In this sense it can
rightly describe the idea of creation as something of no
use to it: by its very methodology, it is founded upon the
compilation of positivistic material, and such a belief has
no place within its scope. At the same time, of course, it
must leave open the question of whether the further inquiry

proposed by faith is per se justified and possible. In any case it may regard this, in terms of a particular concept of science, as extra-scientific, but it cannot rule out the question as a matter of principle or say that man should not address the question of being as such. On the contrary: such ultimate questions will always be indispensable for man, who confronts the ultimate in his very existence and cannot be reduced to what is scientifically demonstrable. But this still leaves us with the problem of whether the idea of creation, being the broader subject, can for its part accept the idea of evolution within its parameters or whether that contradicts its fundamental approach.

Reasons of various sorts seem at first glance to favor the latter argument; after all, the natural scientists and theologians of the first generation who said so were neither foolish nor malicious: on either side they certainly had their reasons, which we must take into account if we do not want to arrive at hasty syntheses that will not withstand challenges or are simply dishonest. The objections that come to mind are of quite different sorts. One can say first, for instance, that belief in creation has been expressed for centuries as faith in the creation of the individual species and in the notion of a static world view; now that this has become untenable, the belief cannot abruptly toss this ballast aside; rather, it has become entirely inapplicable. This objection, which today no longer seems very serious to us, becomes more acute when one reflects that even today faith still necessarily regards the creation of one particular creature as indispensable: the creation of man. For if man is only the product of evolution, then spirit, too, is a random formation. But if spirit evolved, then matter is the primary thing and the sufficient cause of all the rest. And if that is so, then God vanishes and, with him, Creator and creation automatically. But how is man—one among many beings, however excellent and great he may be—to be kept out of the chain of evolutionary developments? Now this shows that the creation of individual creatures and the idea of creation itself cannot be separated quite so readily as it may have appeared at first. For it appears to be a matter of principle here. Either all individual things are the product of evolution, including man. Or else they are not. The second hypothesis is ruled out, and so the first remains; and this appears now, as we have just realized, to call the whole idea of creation into question, because it abolishes the primacy and superiority of spirit, which in some form are to be regarded as a fundamental prerequisite for belief in creation.

Now some have tried to get around this problem by saying that the human body may be a product of evolution, but the soul is not by any means: God himself created it, since spirit cannot emerge from matter. This answer seems to have in its favor the fact that spirit cannot be examined by the same scientific method with which one studies the history of organisms, but only at first glance is this a satisfactory answer. We have to continue the line of questioning: Can we divide man up in this way between theologians and scientists—the soul for the former, the body for the latter? Is that not intolerable for both? The natural scientist believes that he can see the man as a whole gradually taking shape; he also finds an area of psychological transition in which human behavior slowly arises out of animal activity, without being able to draw a clear boundary. (Of course, he lacks the material with which to do so—something that often is not admitted with sufficient clarity.) Conversely, if the theologian is convinced that the soul gives form to the body as well, characterizing it through and through as a human body, so that a human being is spirit only as body and is body only as and in the spirit, then this division of man loses all meaning for him, too.

Indeed, in that case the spirit has created for itself a brand-new body and thereby cancelled out all of evolution. Thus from both perspectives the theme of creation and evolution seems to lead in man's case to a strict either-or that allows for no intermediate positions. Yet, according to the present state of our knowledge, that would probably mean the end of belief in creation.

With that, the beautiful harmony that seemed to stand out clearly on the first level of the inquiry has completely dissolved again, and we are back where we started. How are we to make any progress? Well, a little while ago we had touched upon a middle level that at first seemed unimportant but now could prove to be the center of the inquiry and the starting point for a defensible answer. To what extent is faith bound up with the notion that God created the individual fundamental realities of the world? This way of framing the question may seem at first somewhat superficial, but it follows logically from a general problem that could very well represent the middle stratum of our whole question: Can the notion of a world of becoming be reconciled with the fundamental biblical idea of the creation of the world through the Word, with the derivation of being [*Sein*] from creative meaning [*Sinn*]? Can the idea of being that is expressed therein coexist intellectually with the idea of becoming as outlined in the theory of evolution? Concealed within these questions is another quite fundamental question about the relation between world view and faith in general. This will be a good place to start. For in trying to think at the same time as a believer in creation and as a scientist (that is, according to the theory of evolution), obviously one will attribute to faith a different world view from the one that previously was accepted as the authentic world view of faith. In this process, actually, we even find the heart of the whole matter around which our reflections have been circling: faith is robbed of its world view, which seemed however to be faith itself, and is connected with another. Can one do this without dissolving its identity? That precisely is our problem.

Here it may be somewhat surprising and at the same time liberating to learn that this question was not asked for the first time in our generation. Rather, the theologians in the early Church were confronted in principle with the same task. For the biblical world view, as expressed in the creation accounts of the Old Testament, was by no means their world view; basically it appeared to them just as unscientific as it does to us. Although people often speak simply of "the ancient world view", it is a considerable mistake to do so. Viewed from outside, it may appear unified to us; for those who lived in it, however, the distinctions that seem insignificant to us were decisive. The early creation accounts express the world view of the ancient Near East, especially of Babylon; the Church Fathers lived in the Hellenistic age, to which that world view seemed mythical, prescientific, and in every respect intolerable. One consideration that helped them, and ought to help us, is that the Bible is really a literature that spans a whole millennium. That literary tradition extends from the world view of the Babylonians to the Hellenist world view that shaped the creation passages of the Wisdom literature, which give a picture of the world and of the creation event completely unlike that of the familiar creation accounts in Genesis, which of course are not uniform themselves. The first and the second chapters of this book present largely contrasting images of the course of creation. But this means that, even within the Bible itself, faith and world view are not identical: the faith *makes use* of a world view but does not coincide with it. Over the course of biblical development, this difference was clearly not a theme for reflection but rather was taken for granted: that is the only way to explain the fact that people changed the forms of cosmological speculation in which they portrayed the idea of creation, not only in the various periods of Israel's history, but also within one and the same period of time, without seeing that as a threat to what was actually meant.

The sense of this internal breadth of faith began to disappear when so-called literal exegesis started to gain wide acceptance and many people lost sight of the transcendence of the Word of God with respect to all of the individual forms in which it is expressed. However, at the same time—from around the thirteenth century—the world view also became fixed in a way hitherto unknown, although in its basic form it was by no means a product of biblical thinking but, on the contrary, could only with some effort be reconciled with the fundamental data of biblical faith. It would not be difficult to uncover the pagan roots of that world view, which later on was thought to be the only Christian world view, and to point out the seam by which we can tell even today that faith made use of it, although it could not become identical to it. But we cannot go into that subject here; we must limit ourselves to the positive question, whether belief in creation, which has outlasted so many different world views and at the same time has influenced and leavened them by its critique and thus furthered the development, can continue to exist as a meaningful statement in light of the evolutionary understanding of the world. Now faith was not identical to any one of the previous world views but rather answered a question that leads back behind the world views and then, of course, becomes entrenched in them, and it is clear that faith cannot and should not be identified with our world view either. It would be foolish and untrue to try to pass off evolutionary theory as a product of faith, even though the latter can be said to

have contributed to forming that intellectual world in which
the theory of evolution could come about. It would be
even more foolish to regard faith as a sort of illustration
and corroboration of the theory of evolution. The level of
its questioning and answering is completely different, as we
determined earlier; all that we can try to do is to determine whether the fundamental human question with which
faith is associated can still be legitimately answered, even in
present-day intellectual circumstances, as it is by belief in
creation, and thus in what form the evolutionary world view,
too, may be understood as an expression of creation.

In order to move forward, we must examine more closely
both the creation account and also the idea of evolution;
both of these things, unfortunately, are possible here only
in outline form. Let us ask first, then, starting with the
latter topic: How does one actually understand the world
when it is viewed in evolutionary terms? An essential component, of course, is the notion that being and time enter
into a fixed relation: being *is* time; it does not merely *have*
time. Only in becoming does it exist and unfold into itself.
Accordingly, being is understood dynamically, as being-in-
movement, and it is understood as something directed: it
does not always revolve around the same state of affairs but
rather advances. Admittedly, there is a debate over whether
the concept of progress can be applied to the evolutionary
chain, especially since there is no neutral standard available
that would allow us to say specifically what should be
regarded as better or less good and, consequently, when we
could seriously speak of an advance.

Nevertheless, the special relation that man assumes with
respect to all the rest of reality entitles him to regard himself as the point of reference, at least for the question about
himself: insofar as he is at issue, he is no doubt justified in
doing so. And when he measures in this way, the direction

of evolution and its progressive character are ultimately indisputable, even if one takes into account the fact that there are dead ends in evolution and that its path by no means runs in a straight line. Detours, too, are a path, and by way of detours, too, one arrives at the goal, as evolution itself demonstrates. Of course the question remains open whether being, understood in such fashion as a path—that is, evolution as a whole—has a meaning, and it cannot be decided within the theory of evolution itself; for that theory this is a methodologically foreign question, although, of course, for a live human being it is the fundamental question on which the whole thing depends. Science rightly acknowledges its limits in this regard and declares that this question, which is indispensable for man, cannot be answered within science but only within the framework of a "faith system". We need not be concerned here with the opinion of many people that the Christian "faith system" is unsuited to answering this question and that a new one must be found, because they thereby make a statement within their own faith-decision and outside the parameters of their science.[3]

With that, however, we are now in a position to say precisely what the belief in creation means with regard to the evolutionary understanding of the world. Confronted with the fundamental question, which cannot be answered by evolutionary theory itself, of whether meaninglessness or meaning [Sinn] prevails, this belief expresses the conviction that the world as a whole, as the Bible says, comes from the Logos, that is, from creative mind [Sinn] and represents the temporal form of its self-actuation. From the perspective of our understanding of the world, creation is not a distant beginning or a beginning divided up into several stages,

[3] Cf. W. Bröker, *Der Sinn von Evolution: Ein naturwissenschaftlich-theologischer Diskussionsbeitrag* (Düsseldorf, 1967), esp. 50–58.

but rather it concerns being as something temporal and becoming: temporal being as a whole is encompassed by the one creative act of God, which gives it, in its division, its unity, in which at the same time its meaning consists, a meaning that is unfathomable to us because we do not see the whole but are ourselves only parts of it. Belief in creation does not tell us what the meaning of the world is, but only that there is one: the whole back and forth of being-in-becoming is the free and therefore inherently risky actuation of the primordial creative thought from which it has its being. And so today, perhaps, we can understand better what the Christian dogma of creation was always saying but could hardly bring to bear because of the influence of the model from antiquity: creation should be thought of, not according to the model of the craftsman who makes all sorts of objects, but rather in the manner in which thought is creative. And at the same time it becomes evident that being-in-movement as a whole (and not just the beginning) is creation and that likewise the whole (and not merely what comes later) is, properly speaking, reality and its proper movement. To summarize all this, we can say: To believe in creation means to understand, in faith, the world of becoming revealed by science as a meaningful world that comes from a creative mind.

But this already clearly delineates also the answer to the question about the creation of man, because now the foundational decision about the place of spirit and meaning in the world has been made: the recognition of the world of becoming as the self-actuation of a creative thought includes also its derivation from the creativity of the spirit, from the *Creator Spiritus*. In the writings of Teilhard de Chardin we find the following ingenious comment on this question: "What distinguishes a materialist from a spiritualist is no longer, by any means (as in philosophy, which establishes fixed concepts) the fact that he admits a transition between the physical infrastructure and the psychic superstructure of things, but *only* the fact that he incorrectly sets the *definitive* point of equilibrium in the cosmic movement on the side of the infrastructure, that is, on the side of disintegration." [4] Certainly one can debate the details in this formulation; yet the decisive point seems to me to be grasped quite accurately: the alternative: materialism or a spiritually defined world view, chance or meaning, is presented to us today in the form of the question of whether one regards spirit and life in its ascending forms as an incidental mold on the surface of the material world (that is, of the category of existing things that do not understand themselves), or whether one regards spirit as the goal of the process and, conversely, matter as the prehistory of the spirit. If one chooses the second alternative, it is clear that spirit is not a random product of material developments, but rather that matter signifies a moment in the history of spirit. This, however, is just another way of saying that spirit is created and not the mere product of development, even though it comes to light by way of development.

With that we have reached the point at which we can answer the question of how in fact the theological statement about the special creation of man can coexist with an evolutionary world view or what form it must assume within an evolutionary world view. To discuss this in detail would naturally go beyond the parameters of this essay; a few notes must suffice. We should recall first that, with respect to the creation of man, too, "creation" does not designate a remote beginning but rather has each of us in view along with Adam: every human being *is* directly in relation to God.

---

[4] Cited from Claude Tresmontant, *Einführung in das Denken Teilhard de Chardins* (Freiburg and Munich, 1961), 45.

Faith declares no more about the first man than it does about each one of us, and, conversely, it declares no less about us than it does about the first man.

Every human being is more than the product of inherited traits and environment; no one results exclusively from calculable this-worldly factors; the mystery of creation looms over every one of us. This would then lead to the insight that spirit does not enter the picture as something foreign, as a second substance in addition to matter; the appearance of spirit, according to the previous discussion, means rather that an advancing movement arrives at the goal that has been set for it. Finally, it would have to be noted that precisely the creation of spirit is least of all to be imagined as an artisan activity of God, who suddenly began tinkering with the world.

If creation means dependence of being, then special creation is nothing other than special dependence of being.[5] The statement that man is created in a more specific, more direct way by God than other things in nature, when expressed somewhat less metaphorically, means simply this: that man is willed by God in a specific way, not merely as a being that "is there", but as a being that knows him; not only as a construct that he thought up, but as an existence that can think about him in return. We call the fact that man is specifically willed and known by God his special creation.

From this vantage point, one can immediately make a diagnosis about the form of anthropogenesis: The clay became man at that moment in which a being for the first time was capable of forming, however dimly, the thought "God". The first "thou" that—however stammeringly—was said by

[5] P. Smulders, *Theologie und Evolution: Versuch über Teilhard de Chardin* (Essen, 1963), 96.

human lips to God marks the moment in which spirit arose in the world. Here the Rubicon of anthropogenesis was crossed. For it is not the use of weapons or fire, not new methods of cruelty or of useful activity that constitute man, but rather his ability to be immediately in relation to God. This holds fast to the doctrine of the special creation of man; herein lies the center of belief in creation in the first place. Herein also lies the reason why the moment of anthropogenesis cannot possibly be determined by paleontology: anthropogenesis is the rise of the spirit, which cannot be excavated with a shovel. The theory of evolution does not invalidate faith, nor does it corroborate it. But it does challenge faith to understand itself more profoundly and thus to help man to understand himself and to become increasingly what he is: the being who is supposed to say "thou" to God in eternity.

Jesus

The Only Begotten Son of God

1. The starting point for Christology in the New Testament is the fact of the Resurrection of Jesus Christ from the dead: the Resurrection is God's way of publicly taking the side of Jesus in the proceedings organized by Jews and Gentiles against him. God's defense of him confirms:

a. his interpretation of the Old Testament in opposition to political messianism and to apocalyptic thinking pure and simple; and

b. the claim to divinity on account of which he had been condemned to death.

2. The Resurrection thus makes it possible to interpret the crucifixion of Jesus in terms of the Old Testament concept of the suffering just man that finds its climactic expressions in Psalm 22 (21) and Isaiah 53. This in turn brings in the idea of representation and, as the words of Jesus at the Last Supper indicate, a continuity with the sacrificial tradition of Israel, a tradition that is here linked to Isaiah 53 and reinterpreted in terms of martyrdom: Jesus is the true lamb of sacrifice, the covenant sacrifice in which the deepest meaning of all Old Testament liturgies is fulfilled. Thus the way

Translated by Matthew J. O'Connell and Michael J. Miller.

is cleared for the concept of redemption and for the essential significance of the Christian liturgy.

3. The Resurrection of Jesus is the basis of his abiding lordship. This assertion has two consequences:

a. The Resurrection of Jesus confirms the belief in a general resurrection that had not yet become a clear part of Israel's creed, and thus it provides the basis for the specifically Christian eschatological hope.

b. God's defense of Jesus against the official interpretation of the Old Testament as given by the competent Jewish authorities makes possible in principle that freedom from the letter of the law that will lead to the Church of the pagans.

4. The claim to divinity that the Resurrection of Jesus confirms finds expression in the image of Jesus sitting at the Father's right hand. As a result of the claim, application is made to Jesus of the Old Testament messianic promises that take pointed form in such texts as Psalm 2:7: "You are my son, today I have begotten you." The initially numerous and varied ways of expressing the divinity of Jesus evidently yield priority, as time goes on, to the concepts "Christ" (Messiah) and "Son". These were the ones that corresponded best to the Old Testament promises and to the claim of the historical Jesus as remembered by the community.

5. Constitutive for the faith of the growing Church was the consciousness that in this interpretation of the person of Jesus it was not posthumously bestowing a theological transfiguration upon a teacher in Israel, but was rather interpreting the words and work of Jesus in an objectively correct way. Consequently, the remembrance and retention of the words of Jesus and of the course of his life, especially

his Passion, were from the beginning an essential factor in the formation of Christian tradition and in the norms applied to it. The identity of the earthly with the risen Jesus is fundamental to the faith of the community and rules out any later separation of the historical from the kerygmatic Jesus.

6. The primary function of the formula "You are my son, today I have begotten you" is to interpret the event of the Resurrection; it says, that is, that the Resurrection is the elevation of Jesus to his throne, the proclamation of his kingship and sonship. But since the Resurrection was at the same time seen to be essentially a confirmation of Jesus' claim to divinity, a claim for which he had to undergo death on the Cross (Thesis 1b), it became evident that the title of Son must in principle be applicable to him even before the Resurrection and that it is a valid description of what Jesus was.

7. The implications of all this are brought out with full clarity in the Gospel of John. Here Jesus does not simply proclaim the Word of God; he is himself God's Word in the whole of his existence. In him God acts as a human being. Consequently, it now becomes fully clear that in Jesus two lines of Old Testament promise and expectation converge: the promise of a Savior who is of David's lineage, and a directly theological promise that sees God himself as the ultimate salvation of Israel. At the same time, Jesus' claim to divinity, as handed down in the Synoptic Gospels, here acquires its full context; the words and actions of Jesus in which he in fact presents himself as God become intelligible.

8. Given the increasing reflection on the presuppositions of the Easter event in the person of the earthly Jesus, it is understandable that the traditions regarding the birth and

childhood of Jesus should become part of the official tradition of the Church. The great prophets were called by
God "from their mother's womb", but Jesus, who is superior to the prophets, was actually conceived by the power
of that Spirit who had called the prophets. This already
makes it clear that his consciousness of divine status is not
based on a subsequent call but on what he is from the very
beginning.

9. While the Gospel tradition reports the normative words
and actions of Jesus, the professions of faith elaborated by
the growing Church endeavor to single out the central reference points of the tradition. The process of developing
christological creeds begins with the confessions of faith
associated with the first Easter; it reaches a certain comple-
tion at the Council of Chalcedon. Two main assertions of
this council are to be emphasized:

a. Out of all the christological titles expressing dignity
and rank, which were used from the beginning in the effort
to verbalize the mystery of Christ, the council chooses as
the most normative and comprehensive the designation
"Son of God". This title by now has behind it the whole
weight of belief in the Trinity; it fits in, too, with the
central place of John's Gospel in thinking on Christology.

b. In speaking of two natures and one person, the council is attempting to bring out the paradoxical character of
the title "Son". Jesus is a man and possesses human nature
in the fullest sense. At the same time, he is one with God,
not simply by reason of his conscious dedication to the Lord,
but by reason of his very being. As Son of God he is just as
truly God as he is truly man.

10. The concept of redemption thus acquires its ultimate
theological depth. The being of man is incorporated into

the being of God. But this ontological assertion has meaning only if there is presupposed the concrete, real, loving
human reality of Jesus in whose death the being of the
human person is concretely opened to God and given over
into the possession of God.

Incarnate of the Virgin Mary

"You Are Full of Grace"

Elements of Marian piety according to the Bible

"From henceforth all generations will call me blessed"—
these words of the Mother of Jesus handed on for us by
Luke (Lk 1:48) are at once a prophecy and a charge laid
upon the Church of all times. This phrase from the Magnificat, the spirit-filled prayer of praise that Mary addresses
to the living God, is thus one of the principal foundations
of Christian devotion to her. The Church invented nothing new of her own when she began to extol Mary; she
did not plummet from the worship of the one God to the
praise of man. The Church does what she must; she carries out the task assigned her from the beginning. At the
time Luke was writing this text, the second generation of
Christianity had already arrived, and the "family" of the
Jews had been joined by that of the Gentiles, who had
been incorporated into the Church of Jesus Christ. The
expression "all generations, all families" was beginning to
be filled with historical reality. The Evangelist would certainly not have transmitted Mary's prophecy if it had seemed
to him an indifferent or obsolete item. He wished in his

Translated by Adrian Walker.

Gospel to record "with care" what "the eyewitnesses and ministers of the word" (Lk1:2–3) had handed on from the beginning, in order to give the faith of Christianity, which was then striding onto the stage of world history, a reliable guide for its future course.[1] Mary's prophecy numbered among those elements he had "carefully" ascertained and considered important enough to transmit to posterity. This fact assumes that Mary's words were guaranteed by reality: the first two chapters of Luke's Gospel give evidence of a sphere of tradition in which the remembrance of Mary was cultivated and the Mother of the Lord was loved and praised. They presuppose that the still somewhat naive exclamation of the unnamed woman, "blessed is the womb that bore you" (Lk 11:27), had not entirely ceased to resound but, as Jesus was more deeply understood, had likewise attained a purer form that more adequately expressed its content. They presuppose that Elizabeth's greeting, "blessed are you among women" (Lk 1:42), which Luke characterizes as words spoken in the Holy Spirit (Lk 1:41), had not been a once-only episode. The continued existence of such praise at least in one strand of early Christian tradition is the basis of Luke's infancy narrative. The recording of these words in the Gospel raises this veneration of Mary from historical fact to a commission laid upon the Church of all places and all times.

The Church neglects one of the duties enjoined upon her when she does not praise Mary. She deviates from the word of the Bible when her Marian devotion falls silent. When this happens, in fact, the Church no longer even glorifies God as she ought. For though we do know God by means of his creation—"Ever since the creation of the

---

[1] See F. Mußner, "Καθεξῆς im Lukasprolog", in *Jesus und Paulus*, festschrift for W. G. Kümmel, ed. E. E. Ellis and E. Gräßer, 253–55 (Göttingen, 1975).

world [God's] invisible nature, namely, his eternal power and deity, has been clearly perceived in the things that have been made" (Rom 1:20)—we also know him, and know him more intimately, through the history he has shared with man. Just as the history of a man's life and the relationships he has formed reveal what kind of person he is, God shows himself in a history, in men through whom his own character can be seen. This is so true that he can be "named" through them and identified in them: the God of Abraham, of Isaac, and of Jacob. Through his relation with men, through the faces of men, God has made himself accessible and has shown *his* face. We cannot try to bypass these human faces in order to get to God alone, in his "pure form", as it were. This would lead us to a God of our own invention in place of the real God; it would be an arrogant purism that regards its own ideas as more important than God's deeds. The above-cited verse of the Magnificat shows us that Mary is one of the human beings who in an altogether special way belong to the name of God, so much so, in fact, that we cannot praise him rightly if we leave her out of account. In doing so we forget something about him that must not be forgotten. What, exactly? Our first attempt at an answer could be his maternal side, which reveals itself more purely and more directly in the Son's Mother than anywhere else. But this is, of course, much too general. In order to praise Mary correctly and thus to glorify God correctly, we must listen to all that Scripture and tradition say concerning the Mother of the Lord and ponder it in our hearts. Thanks to the praise of "all generations" since the beginning, the abundant wealth of Mariology has become almost too vast to survey. In this brief meditation, I would like to help the reader reflect anew on just a few of the key words Saint Luke has placed in our hands in his inexhaustibly rich infancy narrative.

Mary, daughter Zion—Mother of believers

Let us begin with the angel's greeting to Mary. For Luke, this is the primordial cell of Mariology that God himself wished to present to us through his messenger, the Archangel Gabriel. Translated literally, the greeting reads thus: "Rejoice, full of grace. The Lord is with you" (Lk 1:28). "Rejoice": At first sight, this word appears to be no more than the formulaic greeting current in the Greek-speaking world, and tradition has consistently translated it as "hail". But looked at against the background of the Old Testament, this formula of greeting takes on a more profound significance. Consider, in fact, that the same word used by Luke appears four times in the Septuagint, where in each case it is an announcement of messianic joy (Zeph 3:14; Joel 2:21; Zech 9:9; Lam 4:21).[2] This greeting marks the beginning of the Gospel in the strict sense; its first word is "joy", the new joy that comes from God and breaks through the world's ancient and interminable sadness. Mary is not merely greeted in some vague or indifferent way; that God greets her and, in her, greets expectant Israel and all of humanity is an invitation to rejoice from the innermost depth of our being. The reason for our sadness is the futility of our love, the overwhelming power of finitude, death, suffering, and falsehood. We are sad because we are left alone in a contradictory world where enigmatic signals of divine goodness pierce through the cracks yet are thrown in doubt by a power of darkness that is either God's responsibility or manifests his impotence.

[2] S. Lyonnet was the first to observe this in his article "Χαῖρε, κεχαριτωμένη", *Biblica* 20 (1939): 131–41. These observations were reprised and further developed by R. Laurentin, *Struktur und Theologie der lukanischen Kindheitsgeschichte* (Stuttgart, 1967), 75ff. On the present state of the debate concerning the interpretation of the angelic salutation, see M. Iglesias, *Los evangelios de la infancia*, vol. 2 (Madrid, 1986), 149–60.

"Rejoice"—what reason does Mary have to rejoice in such a world? The answer is: "The Lord is with you." In order to grasp the sense of this announcement, we must return once more to the Old Testament texts upon which it is based, in particular to Zephaniah. These texts invariably contain a double promise to the personification of Israel, daughter Zion: God will come to save, and he will come to dwell in her. The angel's dialogue with Mary reprises this promise and in so doing makes it concrete in two ways. What in the prophecy is said to daughter Zion is now directed to Mary: she is identified with daughter Zion, she is daughter Zion in person. In a parallel manner, Jesus, whom Mary is permitted to bear, is identified with Yahweh, the living God. When Jesus comes, it is God himself who comes to dwell in her. He is the Savior—this is the meaning of the name Jesus, which thus becomes clear from the heart of the promise. René Laurentin has shown through painstaking textual analyses how Luke has used subtle word play to deepen the theme of God's indwelling. Even early traditions portray God as dwelling "in the womb" of Israel—in the Ark of the Covenant. This dwelling "in the womb" of Israel now becomes quite literally real in the Virgin of Nazareth. Mary herself thus becomes the true Ark of the Covenant in Israel, so that the symbol of the Ark gathers an incredibly realistic force: God in the flesh of a human being, which flesh now becomes his dwelling place in the midst of creation.[3]

The angel's greeting—the center of Mariology not invented by the human mind—has led us to the theological foundation of this Mariology. Mary is identified with daughter Zion, with the bridal people of God. Everything said

[3] Cf. Laurentin, *Struktur und Theologie der lukanischen Kindheitsgeschichte*, 79–82; Iglesias, *Los evangelios de la infancia*, 183ff.

about the *ecclesia* in the Bible is true of her, and vice versa: the Church learns concretely what she is and is meant to be by looking at Mary. Mary is her mirror, the pure measure of her being, because Mary is wholly within the measure of Christ and of God, is through and through his habitation. And what other reason could the *ecclesia* have for existing than to become a dwelling for God in the world? God does not deal with abstractions. He is a person, and the Church is a person. The more each one of us becomes a person, person in the sense of a fit habitation for God, daughter Zion, the more we become one, the more we are the Church, and the more the Church is herself.

The typological identification of Mary and Zion leads us, then, into the depths. This manner of connecting the Old and New Testaments is much more than an interesting historical construction by means of which the Evangelist links promise and fulfillment and reinterprets the Old Testament in the light of what has happened in Christ. Mary is Zion in person, which means that her life wholly embodies what is meant by "Zion". She does not construct a self-enclosed individuality whose principal concern is the originality of its own ego. She does not wish to be just this one human being who defends and protects her own ego. She does not regard life as a stock of goods of which everyone wants to get as much as possible for himself. Her life is such that she is transparent to God, "habitable" for him. Her life is such that she is a place for God. Her life sinks her into the common measure of sacred history, so that what appears in her is, not the narrow and constricted ego of an isolated individual, but the whole, true Israel. This "typological identification" is a spiritual reality; it is life lived out of the spirit of Sacred Scripture; it is rootedness in the faith of the Fathers and at the same time expansion into the height and breadth of the coming promises. We understand why the Bible time and again compares the just man to the tree whose roots drink from the living waters of eternity and whose crown catches and synthesizes the light of heaven.

Let us return once more to the angel's greeting. Mary is called "full of grace". The Greek word for grace (*charis*) derives from the same root as the words joy and rejoice (*chara, chairein*).[4] Thus, we see once more in a different form the same context to which we were led by our earlier comparison with the Old Testament. Joy comes from grace. One who is in the state of grace can rejoice with deep-going, constant joy. By the same token, grace is joy. What is grace? This question thrusts itself upon our text. Our religious mentality has reified this concept much too much; it regards grace as a supernatural something we carry about in our soul. And since we perceive very little of it, or nothing at all, it has gradually become irrelevant to us, an empty word belonging to Christian jargon, which seems to have lost any relationship to the lived reality of our everyday life. In reality, grace is a relational term: it does not predicate something about an I, but something about a connection between I and thou, between God and man. "Full of grace" could therefore also be translated as: "You are full of the Holy Spirit; your life is intimately connected with God." Peter Lombard, the author of what was the universal theological manual for approximately three centuries during the Middle Ages, propounded the thesis that grace and love are identical but that love "is the Holy Spirit". Grace in the proper and deepest sense of the word is not some thing that comes from God; it is God himself.[5] Redemption means that God,

---

[4] Cf. H. Conzelmann, art. "Χάρις, κτλ.", in *ThWNT* 9:363–66.

[5] Peter Lombard, *Sententiae* I, dist. 17, 1. This direct identification of love, grace, and the Holy Spirit was, however, later rejected—and rightly so—by all the great Scholastic doctors. See, for example, Bonaventure's commentary on the *Sentences* I, dist. 17, a. and q. 1; Thomas Aquinas, *S. Th.* II–II,

acting as God truly does, gives us nothing less than himself.
The gift of God is God—he who as the Holy Spirit is communion with us. "Full of grace" therefore means, once again,
that Mary is a wholly open human being, one who has
opened herself entirely, one who has placed herself in God's
hands boldly, limitlessly, and without fear for her own fate.
It means that she lives wholly by and in relation to God.
She is a listener and a prayer, whose mind and soul are alive
to the manifold ways in which the living God quietly calls
to her. She is one who prays and stretches forth wholly to
meet God; she is therefore a lover, who has the breadth
and magnanimity of true love, but who has also its unerr-
ing powers of discernment and its readiness to suffer.

Luke has flooded this fact with the light of yet another
round of motifs. In his subtle way he constructs a parallel
between Abraham, the father of believers, and Mary, the
Mother of believers.[6] To be in a state of grace means: to
be a believer. Faith includes steadfastness, confidence, and

---

q. 23, a. 2. As a matter of fact, the idea of created grace is indispensable,
inasmuch as a relation—a fortiori the God-man relation—does not leave
the person who enters into it unchanged. Only the fact that the relation
finds a place in him and qualifies his being proves that the relation is real.
Accordingly, the point of what I say here is not to advocate a return behind
Thomas and Bonaventure to Peter Lombard or to reprise the polemics of
the Reformers against created grace. My aim, rather, is to underscore emphatically the essentially relational character of grace. Regarding the contemporary state of Catholic theology on this question, see J. Auer, *Das Evangelium
der Gnade*, KKD 5 (Regensburg, 1970), 156–59; H. Schauf, "M. J. Scheeben: De inhabitatione Spiritus Sancti", in *M. J. Scheeben: Teologo cattolico
d'ispirazione tomista*, 237–49 (Vatican City, 1988); concise remarks may also
be found in the recent French edition of the *Summa Theologiae*: Thomas
d'Aquin, *Somme théologique*, vol. 3 (Paris, 1985), 159ff.

[6] See R. Laurentin, *Struktur und Theologie der lukanischen Kindheitsgeschichte*,
98. See also the commented version of *Redemptoris Mater: Mary: God's Yes to
Man* (San Francisco: Ignatius Press, 1988); in my introduction, 24ff., and in
the commentary of H. U. von Balthasar, 167f.

devotion, but also obscurity. When man's relation to God, the soul's open availability for him, is characterized as "faith", this word expresses the fact that the infinite distance between Creator and creature is not blurred in the relation of the human I to the divine thou. It means that the model of "partnership", which has become so dear to us, breaks down when it comes to God, because it cannot sufficiently express the majesty of God and the hiddenness of his working. It is precisely the man who has been opened up entirely into God who comes to accept God's otherness and the hiddenness of his will, which can pierce our will like a sword. The parallel between Mary and Abraham begins in the joy of the promised son but continues apace until the dark hour when she must ascend Mount Moriah, that is, until the crucifixion of Christ. Yet it does not end there; it also extends to the miracle of Isaac's rescue—the Resurrection of Jesus Christ. Abraham, father of faith—this title describes the unique position of the patriarch in the piety of Israel and in the faith of the Church. But is it not wonderful that—without any revocation of the special status of Abraham—a "*Mother* of believers" now stands at the beginning of the new people and that our faith again and again receives from her pure and high image its measure and its path?

Mary as prophetess

With this meditative exegesis of the angelic salutation, we have, so to say, pinpointed the theological locus of Mariology. We have answered the question, "What is the significance of the figure of Mary in the fabric of faith and devotion?" I would now like to illustrate further our fundamental intuition in light of two other aspects of Mary presented in Luke's Gospel.

The first aspect relates to Mary's prayer, to her meditative character. We could also say that it has to do with the
mystical element in her nature, which the Fathers closely
associate with prophecy. I have in mind here three texts in
which this aspect comes clearly to the fore. The first is found
in the context of the Annunciation scene: Mary is dismayed by the angel's greeting—this is the holy dread that
comes upon man when God, the Wholly Other, draws close
to him. She is afraid, and she "considered in her mind what
sort of greeting this might be" (Lk 1:29). The word the
Evangelist uses for "consider" derives from the Greek root
"dialogue". In other words, Mary enters into an interior
dialogue with the Word. She carries on an inner dialogue
with the Word that has been given her; she speaks to it and
lets it speak to her, in order to fathom its meaning.

The second pertinent text occurs after the account of
the adoration of Jesus by the shepherds. There it is said that
Mary "kept", "held together", and "placed together" all
these words (= "happenings") "in her heart" (Lk 2:19). The
Evangelist here ascribes to Mary the insightful, meditative
remembrance that in the Gospel of John will play such an
important role in the unfolding of the message of Jesus in
the Church under the working of the Spirit. Mary sees the
events as "words", as happenings full of meaning because
they come from God's meaning-creating will. She translates
the events into words and penetrates them, bringing them
into her "heart"—into that interior dimension of understanding where sense and spirit, reason and feeling, interior
and exterior perception interpenetrate circumincessively. She
is thus able to see the totality without getting lost in individual details and to understand the points of the whole.
Mary "puts together", "holds together"—she fits the single
details into the whole picture, compares and considers them,
and then preserves them. The word becomes seed in good

soil. She does not snatch at it, hold it locked in an imme-
diate, superficial grasp, and then forget it. Rather, the outward event finds in her heart a space to abide and, in this
way, gradually to unveil its depth, without any blurring of
its once-only contours.

There is an analogous statement in connection with the
scene centering on the twelve-year-old Jesus in the Temple. The first stage is "they did not understand the saying
which he spoke to them" (Lk 2:50). Even for the believing
man who is entirely open to God, the words of God are
not comprehensible and evident right away. Those who
demand that the Christian message be as immediately understandable as any banal statement hinder God. Where there
is no humility to accept the mystery, no patience to receive
interiorly what one has not yet understood, to carry it to
term, and to let it open at its own pace, the seed of the
word has fallen on rocky ground; it has found no soil. Even
the Mother does not understand the Son at this moment,
but once again she "kept all these things in her heart" (Lk
2:51). The Greek term for "keep" here is not precisely the
same as the one Luke uses after the scene with the shepherds.
Whereas the latter emphasizes more the aspect of "together",
of unifying contemplation, the former stresses the element
of "through", of carrying the word to term and holding it
fast.

Behind this portrayal of Mary, we glimpse the picture
of the godly man of the Old Testament as he is described
by the psalms, especially the great psalm of God's word,
Psalm 119. In the picture that emerges there of the pious
man, it is characteristic for him to love God's word, to carry
it in his heart, ponder over it, contemplate it by day and
by night, and be wholly imbued with it and permeated by
its life. The Fathers summed this up in a beautiful and
eloquent image, which we find formulated, for example,

by Theodotus of Ancyra in the following terms: "The Virgin has given birth ... the Prophetess has borne a child. ... It was through hearing that Mary, the prophetess, conceived the living God. For the natural path of discourse is the ear."[7] Mary's divine maternity and her enduring attitude of openness to God's word are seen as interpenetrating here: giving ear to the angel's greeting, Mary welcomes the Holy Spirit into herself. Having become pure hearing, she receives the Word so totally that it becomes flesh in her. This understanding of hearing, meditation, and conception appears in conjunction with the concept and the reality of prophecy: inasmuch as Mary hears in the very depths of her heart, so that she truly interiorizes the Word and can give it to the world in a new way, she is a prophetess. Alois Grillmeier has offered the following commentary on this patristic reflection:

> We see in the image of "Mary the prophetess", for example, no trace of pagan divination. Mary is no Pythia. When we look at the scene of the Annunciation ... and the meeting in Zechariah's house in tandem, prophecy's center of gravity shifts away from the ecstatic to the interior dimension of grace. ... If a place fittingly belongs to Mary in the history of mysticism, her role therein has one meaning: she does nothing but draw away from the periphery and toward the interior essence.[8]

In this way, Mary illustrates the new and specifically Christian understanding of the prophet: life in holiness and truth, which is the true prediction of the future and the only valid

[7] Homily 4, *In Deiparum et Simeonem*, 2 (PG 77, 1392CD). See on this point the important article of A. Grillmeier, "Maria Prophetin", in *Mit ihm und in ihm: Christologische Forschungen und Perspektiven* (Freiburg, 1975), 198–216; citation, 207f.

[8] Grillmeier, *Mit ihm und in ihm*, 215f.

interpretation of every present. In Mary the true greatness
and the surpassing simplicity of Christian mysticism become
visible: not in extraordinary phenomena, in raptures and
visions, but in the abiding exchange of creaturely existence
with the Creator, so that the creature becomes ever more
pervious to him, truly one with him in a holy union at
once bridal and maternal.

No one should try to psychologize the Bible. But perhaps we may, in spite of that, look for the delicate traces in
which the Bible concretizes this way of being in its image
of Mary. For me, the story of the marriage at Cana is one
such instance. Mary is rebuffed. The Lord's hour is not yet
come, whereas the present hour, the period of Jesus' public
activity, requires that she withdraw and keep silence. It appears
strange, almost contradictory, that in spite of this she turns
to the servants and says, "Do whatever he tells you" (Jn
2:5). Is this not simply her inner readiness to let Jesus act,
her intuitive sensitivity to the hidden mystery of the hour?
The second example is Pentecost. The time of Jesus' public
activity had been for her the time of rejection, the time of
darkness. The scene of Pentecost, however, reprises the beginning of the story in Nazareth and shows how the whole
hangs together. Just as Christ had at that time been born of
the Holy Spirit, so now the Church is born by the working of the same Spirit. But Mary is in the midst of those
who pray and wait (Acts 1:16). That prayerful recollection
we identified as characteristic of her nature once again
becomes the space in which the Holy Spirit can enter and
bring about a new creation.

Finally, I would like to refer once more to the Magnificat, which seems to me a sort of recapitulation of all
these aspects. It is above all here, particularly in the prediction that all generations will praise her, that Mary reveals
herself in the eyes of the Fathers to be the Spirit-filled

prophetess.[9] Yet this prophetic prayer is woven entirely of threads from the Old Testament. How many stages led up to the text prior to Christianity, how far the Evangelist was involved in its formulation, are ultimately entirely secondary questions. Luke and the tradition from which he emerges hear in the Magnificat the voice of Mary, the Mother of the Lord. They know that this is how she spoke.[10] She lived so deeply immersed in the word of the Old Covenant that it quite spontaneously became her own. She had lived and prayed through the Bible so deeply, she had "kept it together" in her heart to such a degree, that she saw in its word her life and the life of the world; it was so much her own that she found in it the strength to respond to her hour. God's word had become her own word, and she had surrendered her own word entirely into his: the frontiers were abolished, because her existence, as a lived penetration into the Word, was an existence in the realm of the Holy Spirit. "My soul magnifies the Lord." This does not mean that we can add anything to God, Saint Ambrose says, in commenting on this verse, but that we let him be great in us. To magnify the Lord means, not to want to magnify ourselves, our own name, our own ego; not to spread ourselves and take up more space, but to give him room so that he may be more present in the world. It means to become more truly what we are: not a self-enclosed monad that displays nothing but itself, but God's image. It means to get free of the dust and soot that obscures and begrimes the transparency of the image and to become truly human by pointing exclusively to him.

[9] Ibid., 207–13.

[10] On the dispute surrounding the Magnificat, see H. Schürmann, *Das Lukasevangelium*, vol. 1 (Freiburg, 1969), 71–80; M. Iglesias, *Los cánticos del Evangelio de la infancia según San Lucas* (Madrid, 1983), 61–117.

Mary in the Paschal Mystery

This brings me to the second aspect of the figure of Mary I would like to mention. To magnify God: this means, as we were saying, to free ourselves for him. It signifies the true exodus, man's exodus from himself, that Maximus the Confessor matchlessly describes in his interpretation of Christ's Passion as the "transition between the two wills from opposition to union", a passage leading "through the sacrifice of obedience".[11] Luke's first express mention of the Cross as an aspect of Mary's grace, prophecy, and mysticism occurs in her encounter with the aged Simeon. The old man says to her in prophetic language: "Behold, this child is set for the fall and rising of many in Israel, and for a sign that is spoken against (and a sword will pierce through your own soul also)" (Lk 2:34–35). I am reminded here of Nathan's prophecy to David after the latter's fall into sin: "You . . . have slain [Uriah the Hittite] with the sword of the Ammonites. Now therefore the sword shall never depart from your house" (2 Sam 12:9–10). The sword that hangs over David's house now strikes Mary's heart. In the true David, Christ, and in his Mother, the pure Virgin, the curse is suffered through and overcome.

The sword shall pierce her heart—this statement foreshadows the Son's Passion, which will become her own passion. This passion already begins with her next visit to the Temple: she must accept the precedence of Jesus' true Father and of his house, the Temple; she must learn to release the Son she has borne. She must complete the Yes to God's will that made her a mother by withdrawing into the background and letting Jesus enter upon his mission. Jesus' rebuffs during his public life and her withdrawal are an important

step that will reach its goal on the Cross with the words
"behold, your son." It is no longer Jesus but the disciple
who is her son. To accept and to be available is the first
step required of her; to let go and to release is the second.
Only in this way does her motherhood become complete:
the "blessed is the womb that bore you" comes true only
when it enters into the other beatitude: "Blessed rather are
those who hear the word of God and keep it" (Lk 11:27–
28). By this means Mary is prepared for the mystery of the
Cross, which does not simply end on Golgotha. Her Son
remains a sign of contradiction, and she is thus kept to the
very end in the pain of this contradiction, in the pain of
her messianic motherhood.

The image of the grieving [*leidend*] Mother, who in her
suffering had become sheer compassion [*Mitleid*] and who
now holds the dead Christ on her lap, has become especially dear to Christian piety. In the compassionate Mother,
sufferers of all ages have found the purest reflection of the
divine compassion that is the only true consolation. For,
looked at in its deepest essence, all pain, all suffering is solitude, loss of love, the wrecked happiness of the rejected.
Only the "com", the "with", can heal pain.

In Bernard of Clairvaux we find the wonderful statement that God cannot suffer [*leiden*], but he can suffer with
[be com–passionate, *mit-leiden*].[12] With these words, Bernard

---

[12] *In Cant.* 26, 5 (PL 183, 906): "Impassibilis est Deus, sed non incom-
passibilis" (God is impassible, but not incompassionable). Cf. Henri de Lubac,
History and Spirit: The Understanding of Scripture according to Origen, trans. Anne
Englund Nash and Juvenal Merriell of the Oratory (San Francisco: Ignatius
Press, 2007). The whole section entitled "The God of Origen" (259–80) is
important for this question. This brings us to the problem of "the pain of
God"; H. U. von Balthasar has developed his position on this subject in sev-
eral places, most recently in *Theo-Drama: Theological Dramatic Theory*, vol. 5,
The Last Act, trans. Graham Harrison (San Francisco: Ignatius Press, 1998),
212–34.

brings to a certain conclusion the Fathers' struggle to articulate the newness of the Christian concept of God. Ancient
thought considered the passionlessness [*Leidenschaftslosigkeit*]
of pure intellect to be an essential attribute of God. It proved
difficult for the Fathers to reject this notion and to think of
"passion" [*Leidenschaft*] in God. Yet in the light of the Bible
they saw quite plainly that "Biblical revelation ... upsets
[everything] ... the world had thought about God." They
saw that there is an intimate passion in God, indeed, that it
even constitutes his true essence: love. And because he loves,
suffering [*Leid*] in the form of compassion [*Mitleid*] is not
foreign to him. In this connection, Origen writes: "In his
love for man, the Impassible One has suffered a passion of
mercy." [13] We could say that the Cross of Christ is God's
compassionate suffering with the world. The Hebrew text
of the Old Testament does not draw on psychology to speak
about God's compassionate suffering with man. Rather, in
accordance with the concreteness of Semitic thought, it designates it with a word whose basic meaning refers to a bodily
organ, namely, *rah^amim*. Taken in the singular, *rah^amim* means
the mother's womb. Just as "heart" stands for feeling, and
"loins" and "kidneys" stand for desire and pain, the womb
becomes the term for being with another; it becomes the
deepest reference to man's capacity to stand for another, to
take the other into himself, to suffer him [*erleiden*], and in
this long-suffering to give him life. The Old Testament,
with a word taken from the language of the body, tells us
how God shelters us in himself, how he bears us in himself
with compassionate love. [14]

[13] De Lubac, *History and Spirit*, 277.

[14] Important on this point is the long n. 52 in Pope John Paul II's encyclical *Dives in Misericordia*; see also n. 61. See in addition H. Köster's article
on "Σπλάγχνον κτλ.", in *ThWNT* 7:548–59. It is interesting that in the text
cited above, Origen uses the word σπλαγχνισθῆναι for God's "suffering",

The languages into which the Gospel entered when it came to the pagan world did not have such modes of expression. But the image of the *Pietà*, the Mother grieving [*leidend*] for her Son, became the vivid translation of this word: in her, God's maternal affliction [*Leiden*] is open to view. In her we can behold it and touch it. She is the *compassio* of God, displayed in a human being who has let herself be drawn wholly into God's mystery. It is because human life is at all times suffering that the image of the suffering Mother, the image of the *raḥᵃmim* of God, is of such importance for Christianity. The *Pietà* completes the picture of the Cross, because Mary is the accepted Cross, the Cross communicating itself in love, the Cross that now allows us to experience in her compassion the compassion of God. In this way the Mother's affliction is Easter affliction, which already inaugurates the transformation of death into the redemptive being-with of love. Only apparently have we distanced ourselves from the "rejoice" with which the narrative of Mary begins. For the joy announced to her is not the banal joy clung to in forgetfulness of the abysses of our being and so condemned to plunge into the void. It is the real joy that gives us the courage to venture the exodus of love into the burning holiness of God. It is the true joy that pain does not destroy but first brings to its maturity. Only the joy that stands the test of pain and is stronger than affliction is authentic.

"All generations will call me blessed." We call Mary blessed with words woven together from the angelic salutation and

thus characterizing it as a compassion that is not in contradiction to God's impassibility [*Leidlosigkeit*]. A propos of this, Köster, "Σπλάγχνον κτλ.", 550, calls attention to the fact that the Septuagint commonly translates *raḥᵃmim*, not as σπλάγχνα (bowels), but as οἰκτιρμοί (compassion). The translators thus replace the image, which they perceive as too crude, with the point it is meant to convey: "compassion".

Elizabeth's greeting—that is, with words not of human invention. The Evangelist tells us, in fact, that Elizabeth uttered her greeting filled with the Holy Spirit. "Blessed are you among women, and blessed is the fruit of your womb": these are the words of Elizabeth, which we repeat after her. Blessed are you—God's promise to Abraham resounds once more at the beginning of the New Covenant: "You will be a blessing ... and by you all the families of the earth shall bless themselves" (Gen 12:2–3). Mary, who recapitulated the faith of Abraham and brought it to its goal, is now the one blessed. She has become the Mother of believers, through whom all the generations and races of the earth obtain blessing. We place ourselves in this blessing when we praise her. We enter into it when, together with her, we become believers who magnify God because he dwells among us as "God with us": Jesus Christ, the true and only Redeemer of the world.

He Was Crucified, Suffered Death, and Was Buried

Good Friday

I

In the great *Passions* by Johann Sebastian Bach that stir us anew each year during Holy Week, the awful event of Good Friday is bathed in transfigured and transfiguring beauty. Admittedly, these *Passions* do not speak of the Resurrection— they end with the burial of Jesus—but their purity and nobility are derived from the certainty of Easter, the certainty of a hope that is not extinguished even in the night of death.

Nowadays, however, this confident and tranquil faith that does not need to speak of the Resurrection, because it lives and thinks in its light, has become strangely alien to us. In the *Passion* of the Polish composer Krzysztof Penderecki the tranquility of a community of believers who live constantly in the light of Easter has disappeared. Instead, we hear the tortured cry of the persecuted at Auschwitz; the cynicism and brutal commando voices of the masters of that hell; the eager voices of the hangers-on as they join in the screeching, thus hoping to rescue themselves from the terror; the

Translated by Matthew J. O'Connell and Michael J. Miller.

lashing whips of the anonymous, omnipresent power of darkness; the hopeless sighs of the dying.

This is the Good Friday of the twentieth century: The face of man is mocked, covered with spittle, beaten by man himself. From the gas chambers of Auschwitz, from the ruined villages and outraged children of Vietnam; from the slums of India, Africa, and Latin America; from the concentration camps of the Communist world that Solzhenitsyn has brought before our eyes with such passionate intensity: from every side the "bleeding head so wounded, reviled and put to scorn" gazes at us with a realism that makes a mockery of any aesthetic transfiguration. If Kant and Hegel had been right, the progress of the Enlightenment should have made man ever freer, more reasonable, and more upright. Instead, the demons we had so eagerly declared dead rise ever more powerfully from the depths of human beings and teach them to feel a profound anxiety at their own power and powerlessness: their power to destroy, their powerlessness to find themselves and master their own inhumanity.

The most terrible moment in the story of Jesus' Passion is doubtless the one in which he cries aloud in his extreme torment on the Cross: "My God, my God, why have you forsaken me?" The words are from a psalm in which Israel—suffering, oppressed, scorned because of its faith—cries out its need before the face of God. But this cry of supplication, uttered by a people whose election and communion with God seem to have turned into a curse, acquires its full dreadfulness on the lips of him who is himself the redemptive nearness of God in the midst of men. If *he* is conscious of being abandoned by God, then where is God still to be found? Does this moment not mark, in all truth, the darkening of the sun of history, the hour in which the light of the world is extinguished? Today, the echo of this cry, magnified a thousandfold, rings in our ears from the hell of the concentration camps, from the battlefields of the guerilla wars, from the slums of the starving and despairing: "Where are you, God, that you could create such a world, that you can look on while your most innocent creatures often suffer the most terribly, as sheep are led to the slaughter and cannot open their mouths?"

Job's ancient question has acquired an edge hardly ever matched in the past. Often, of course, the question is asked rather arrogantly, and behind it can be glimpsed a sense of malicious satisfaction, as when student newspapers repeat in overbearing tones what the students have had preached to them: that in a world forced to learn the names of Auschwitz and Vietnam no one can seriously talk any longer of a "good" God. But the insincerity that is all too often evident does not make the questions any less a valid one. For in this our own hour of history we all seem for practical purposes to be contemporaries of Jesus at the point when his Passion turned into a cry to the Father for help: "My God, my God, why have you forsaken me?"

What can we say in response to this cry? In the last analysis, the question Jesus asked is not to be answered with words and arguments, for it penetrates to a depth unfathomable to mere reason and the words that such reason produces. The failure of Job's friends is the inevitable lot of all who believe they can answer the question, positively or negatively, with clever thoughts and words. No, the question can only be endured, suffered through—with him and at the side of him who suffered it to the end for all of us and with all of us. An arrogant sense of having dealt adequately with it—whether in the spirit of the student newspaper or in the spirit of theological apologetics—can only miss the real point.

It is possible, nonetheless, to make a couple of suggestions. The first thing to be noted is that Jesus does not declare the absence of God but rather turns it into a prayer.

If we want to unite the Good Friday of the twentieth century with the Good Friday of Jesus, we must integrate our century's cry of distress with Jesus' cry to the Father for help and transform it into a prayer to God, who is nevertheless near to us. You may, of course, go a step farther and ask: "Is it possible to pray honestly as long as we have done nothing to wipe the blood from those who have been beaten and to dry their tears? Is Veronica's gesture not the least that must be made before there can be any talk of prayer? Can one pray at all with the lips alone, or does that not always require the whole person?"

But let us be content with this first suggestion, which leads us to reflect on a second one: Jesus has truly entered into and shared the affliction of the condemned, while we—most of us, at least—have on the whole been only more or less involved onlookers at the horrors of the twentieth century. This fact is connected with an observation of some importance: Remarkably enough, the claim that there can no longer be any God, the claim, that is, that God has completely disappeared, is the urgent conclusion drawn by *onlookers* at the terror, the people who view the horrors from the cushioned armchair of their own prosperity and attempt to pay their tribute to it and ward it off from themselves by saying, "If such things can happen, there is no God!"

But among those who are themselves immersed in the terrible reality, the effect is not infrequently just the opposite: it is precisely then that they discover God. In this world of suffering, adoration has continued to rise up from the fiery furnaces of the crematories and not from the spectators of the horror. It is no accident that the people who in their history have been the most condemned to suffering, the people who have been the worst battered and the most wretched and who did not have to wait for 1940–1945 to be in "Auschwitz", also became the people of revelation, the people who have known God and made him visible to the world. And it is no accident that the man who has been the most afflicted and has suffered most—Jesus of Nazareth—was and is the revealer, indeed, revelation itself. It is no accident that faith in God flows from a "head so wounded", from a crucified man, and that atheism has Epicurus for father and originates in the world of the satisfied onlooker.

The awful and threatening gravity of a saying of Jesus that we usually set aside as inappropriate suddenly comes home to us here: A camel will sooner pass through the eye of a needle than a rich man enter the kingdom of heaven. Rich man? That means anyone who is well-off, saturated with prosperity, and knows suffering only from television. We should not be too ready to dismiss these words of Jesus, which are a warning to us, especially on Good Friday. Admittedly, we need not and indeed must not call down suffering and affliction on ourselves. Good Friday is something God imposes when and where he wishes. But we ought to learn even more fully—not only theoretically but in our practical lives—that every good thing is a gift on loan from him and that we must account for it before him. We must also learn— again, not just theoretically, but in the way we think and act—that in addition to the Real Presence of Jesus in the Church and in the Blessed Sacrament there is that other, second real presence of Jesus in the least of our brethren, in the downtrodden of this world, in the humblest of human beings; he wants us to find him in all of them. To accept this truth ever anew is the decisive challenge that Good Friday presents to us year after year.

II

The image of the crucified Christ that stands at the center of the Good Friday liturgy reveals the full seriousness of human affliction, human forlornness, human sin. And yet down through the centuries of Church history, the crucifix has constantly been seen as an image of consolation and hope.

Matthias Grünewald's *Isenheimer Altar*, perhaps the most deeply moving painting of the crucifixion that Christendom possesses, stood in a monastery of the Antonian Hospitalers, where people were cared for who had fallen victim to the dreadful plagues that afflicted the West in the late Middle Ages. The crucified Jesus is depicted as one of these people, his whole body marred by plague boils, the most horrible torment of the age. In him the words of the prophet are fulfilled, that he would bear our griefs and carry our sorrows.

Before this image the monks prayed, along with their sick who found consolation in the knowledge that in Christ God suffered with them. This picture helped them realize that precisely by their illness they were identified with the crucified Christ, who in his affliction had become one with all the afflicted of history. In their cross they experienced the presence of the crucified Jesus and knew that in their distress they were being drawn into Christ and thereby into the abyss of everlasting mercy. They experienced his Cross as their redemption.[1]

In our day many have grown deeply mistrustful of this understanding of redemption. Following Karl Marx, they see the consolation of heaven in recompense for the earthly vale of tears as an empty promise that brings no improvement but only renders permanent the world's wretched state and, in the last analysis, benefits only those in whose interest it is to preserve the status quo. Instead of heavenly consolation, then, these people call for changes that will remove

---

[1] See A. Zacharias, *Kleine Kunstgeschichte abendländischer Stile* (Munich, 1957), 132.

and, in this sense, redeem suffering. Not redemption through suffering, but redemption from suffering is their watchword: not expectation of help from God, but the humanization of human beings by their fellows is the task for which they call.

Now of course one could immediately retort that this sets up a false dilemma. The Antonians quite obviously did not see in the Cross of Christ an excuse for not engaging in organized humanitarian aid addressed to special needs. By means of 369 hospitals throughout Europe, they built a network of charitable institutions in which the Cross of Christ was regarded as a very practical summons to seek him in suffering human beings and to heal his wounded body; in other words, to change the world and put an end to suffering.[2]

We may ask, moreover, whether amid all the impressive talk about humaneness and humanization that we hear around us there is as real an impulse to serve and assist as there was in those days. One frequently has the impression that we want to buy our freedom from a task that has become too burdensome for us by at least talking about it; in any case, we get along today in large measure by borrowing people for service roles from the poorer nations, because in our own country the impulse to serve has grown weak. But still we must ask how long a social organism can survive when one of its key organs is failing and can hardly be replaced over the long term by transplantation.

Admittedly, then, even—and especially—with regard to the activity required if we are to shape and transform the world, we must disregard the facile contrasts that are fashionable today and view the question differently. But by doing that, we have still not fully answered the questions we are

---

[2] See K. Hofmann, article "Antonianer" in *Lexikon für Theologie und Kirche* 1:677.

discussing here. For in fact the Antonians followed the Christian creed in preaching and practicing not only redemption from the cross but also redemption through the cross. To do so is to bring out a dimension of human existence that increasingly eludes us today but nonetheless constitutes the very heart of Christianity; in its light alone are we to understand Christian activity for and in this world.

How can we come to see this heart of the matter? I will try to suggest a way by referring to the development of the image of the Cross in the work of a modern artist who, though not a Christian, was increasingly fascinated by the figure of the Crucified and was constantly trying to grasp the essence of it. I am referring to Marc Chagall.[3] He first depicts the crucified Jesus in a very early work that was painted in 1912. Here the entire composition forces us to think of him as a child; he represents the suffering of the innocent, the undeserved suffering in this world that by its very nature is a sign of hope. Then the crucified Jesus disappears completely from Chagall's work for twenty-five years; he reappears only in 1937, but now he conveys a new and more profound meaning.

This triptych on the crucifixion had a remarkable predecessor, another tripartite painting that Chagall later destroyed but of which an oil sketch in colors has survived. That earlier picture was entitled *Revolution*. On the left there is an excited crowd waving red flags and brandishing weapons; by this means the revolution as such is brought into the picture. The right side contains images of peace and joy: the sun, love, music; the idea is that the revolution will produce a transformed, redeemed, restored world. In the center, linking the two halves, is a man doing a handstand.

---

[3] For the following description, cf. H.-M. Rotermund, *Marc Chagall und die Bibel* (Lahr, 1970), 111–38.

Clearly there is a direct allusion to Lenin, the man who symbolizes the entire revolution that turns things upside down and transforms left into right; the kind of total change that leads to a new world is taking place.

The picture recalls a Gnostic text from the early Christian period in which it is said that Adam, that is, mankind, stands on his head and thus causes up and down, left and right, to be reversed; a complete conversion of values—a revolution—is needed if man and the world are to become what they should be. We might call this picture by Chagall a kind of altar to political theology. Just as he had expected the Russian Revolution of 1917 to produce salvation, so after this first disillusionment, he placed his hopes a second time in the French Popular Front that had come into power in 1937.

The fact that Chagall destroyed this picture shows that he buried his hopes a second time and probably for good. He painted a new triptych that has the same structure: on the right, a picture of the salvation that is coming, but purer and less ambivalent than before; on the left, the world in turmoil, but now marked more by suffering than by conflict, and with the crucified Jesus hovering over it. The decisive change, and one that gives a new meaning to the two side panels, is to be found at the center: replacing the symbol of the revolution and its delusive hopes is the colossal image of the crucified Jesus. The rabbi, representing the Old Testament and Israel, who had previously sat at Lenin's side as if in confirmation of his work, is now at the foot of the Cross. The crucified Jesus, and not Lenin, is now the hope of Israel and the world.

We need not inquire to what extent Chagall in his own mind was intending to adopt the Christian interpretation of the Old Testament, of history, and of being human in general. Quite independently of the answer to this question, anyone who sees the two pictures side by side can derive an unambiguously Christian statement from them. The salvation of the world does not come, in the final analysis, from a transformation of the world or a political system that sets itself up as absolute and divine.

We must, indeed, go on working to transform the world, soberly, realistically, patiently, humanely. But mankind has a demand and a question that go beyond anything politics and economics can provide, that can be answered only by the crucified Christ, the man in whom our suffering touches the heart of God and his everlasting love. Indeed, man thirsts for this love; without it he remains an absurd experiment despite all the improvements that can and should be made.

The consolation that goes forth from him who bears the stripes meant for us is something we still need today, in fact, today more than ever. In all truth, he is the only consolation that never degenerates into an empty promise. God grant that we may have eyes to see and a heart open to this consolation; that we may be able to live within it and pass it on to others; that during the Good Friday of history we may receive the Easter mystery that is at work in Christ's Good Friday and, thus, be redeemed.

Descent into Hell—
Ascension—Resurrection
of the Body

Difficulties with the Apostles' Creed

The following reflections are not meant to address the extensive exegetical, religious-historical, dogmatic, and hermeneutical questions connected with the articles from the Creed at issue here. That would be to wander in a primeval forest from which there would be no quick escape. They are an attempt, rather, to uncover the spiritual core of the statements in question after the manner of a meditation and, thus, to lead to the things that really matter in the Creed, beyond all specialized knowledge.

1. "Descended into hell"

Possibly no article of the Creed is so far from present-day attitudes of mind as this one. Together with the belief in the birth of Jesus from the Virgin Mary and that in the Ascension of the Lord, it seems to call most of all for "demythologization", a process that in this case looks devoid of danger

Translated by J. R. Foster and Michael J. Miller.

and unlikely to provoke opposition. The few places where Scripture seems to say anything about this matter (1 Pet 3:19f.; 4:6; Eph 4:9; Rom 10:7; Mt 12:40; Acts 2:27, 31) are so difficult to understand that they can easily be expounded in many different ways. Thus, if in the end one eliminates the statement altogether, one seems to have the advantage of getting rid of a curious idea, and one difficult to harmonize with our own modes of thought, without making oneself guilty of a particularly disloyal act. But is anything really gained by this? Or has one simply evaded the difficulty and obscurity of reality? One can try to deal with problems either by denying their existence or by facing up to them. The first method is the more comfortable one, but only the second leads anywhere. Instead of pushing the question aside, then, should we not learn to see that this article of faith, which liturgically is associated with Holy Saturday in the Church's year, is particularly close to our day and is to a particular degree the experience of our [twentieth] century? On Good Friday our gaze remains fixed on the crucified Christ, but Holy Saturday is the day of the "death of God", the day that expresses the unparalleled experience of our age, anticipating the fact that God is simply absent, that the grave hides him, that he no longer awakes, no longer speaks, so that one no longer needs to gainsay him but can simply overlook him. "God is dead, and we have killed him." This saying of Nietzsche's belongs linguistically to the tradition of Christian Passiontide piety; it expresses the content of Holy Saturday, "descended into hell".[1]

This article of the Creed always reminds me of two scenes in the Bible. The first is that cruel story in the Old Testament

---

[1] Cf. H. de Lubac, *The Drama of Atheist Humanism*, trans. Edith M. Riley, Anne Englund Nash, and Mark Sebanc (San Francisco: Ignatius Press, 1995), 42–58.

in which Elijah challenges the priests of Baal to implore their God to give them fire for their sacrifice. They do so, and naturally nothing happens. He ridicules them, just as the "enlightened rationalist" ridicules the pious person and finds him laughable when nothing happens in response to his prayers. Elijah calls out to the priests that perhaps they had not prayed loud enough: "Cry aloud, for he [Baal] is a god; either he is musing, or has gone aside, or he is on a journey, or perhaps he is asleep and must be awakened" (1 Kings 18:27). When one reads today this mockery of the devotees of Baal, one can begin to feel uncomfortable; one can get the feeling that we have now arrived in that situation and that the mockery must now fall on us. No calling seems to be able to awaken God. The rationalist seems entitled to say to us, "Pray louder, perhaps your God will then wake up." "Descended into hell"; how true this is of our time, the descent of God into muteness, into the dark silence of the absent.

But alongside the story of Elijah and its New Testament analogue, the story of the Lord sleeping in the midst of the storm on the lake (Mk 4:35–41, par.), we must put the Emmaus story (Lk 24:13–35). The disturbed disciples are talking of the death of their hope. To them, something like the death of God has happened: the point at which God finally seemed to have spoken has disappeared. The One sent by God is dead, and so there is a complete void. Nothing replies any more. But while they are there speaking of the death of their hope and can no longer see God, they do not notice that this very hope stands alive in their midst; that "God", or rather the image they had formed of his promise, had to die so that he could live on a larger scale. The image they had formed of God, and into which they sought to compress him, had to be destroyed, so that over the ruins of the demolished house, as it were, they could see the sky again and him who remains the infinitely greater. The German Romantic poet Eichendorff formulated the idea—in the comfortable, to us almost too harmless fashion of his age—like this:

> Du bist's, der, was wir bauen,
> Mild über uns zerbricht,
> Dass wir den Himmel schauen—
> Darum so klag' ich nicht.[2]

Thus the article about the Lord's descent into hell reminds us that not only God's speech but also his silence is part of the Christian revelation. God is not only the comprehensible word that comes to us; he is also the silent, inaccessible, uncomprehended, and incomprehensible ground that eludes us. To be sure, in Christianity there is a primacy of the *logos*, of the word, over silence; God *has* spoken. God *is* word. But this does not entitle us to forget the truth of God's abiding concealment. Only when we have experienced him as silence may we hope to hear his speech, too, which proceeds in silence.[3] Christology reaches out beyond the Cross, the moment when the divine love is tangible, into the death, the silence, and the eclipse of God. Can we wonder that the Church and the life of the individual are led again and again into this hour of silence,

---

[2] "Thou art he who gently breaks about our heads what we build, so that we can see the sky—therefore I have no complaint."—TRANS.

[3] Cf. the significance of silence in the writings of Ignatius of Antioch: *Epistola ad Ephesios* 19, 1: "And to the prince of this world the virginity of Mary and her confinement remained hidden, likewise also the death of the Lord—three loudly calling secrets that were accomplished in God's peace." Quoted by J. A. Fischer, *Die Apostolischen Väter* (Darmstadt, 1956), 157; cf. *Epistola ad Magnesios* 8, 2, which speaks of the λόγος ἀπὸ σιγῆς προελθών (the word that comes from silence), and the meditation on speech and silence in the *Epistola ad Ephesios* 15, 1. On the historical background, H. Schlier, *Religionsgeschichtliche Untersuchungen zu den Ignatiusbriefen* (Berlin, 1929).

into the forgotten and almost discarded article, "Descended
into hell"?

When one ponders this, the question of the "scriptural
evidence" solves itself; at any rate in Jesus' death cry, "My
God, my God, why have you forsaken me?" (Mk 15:34),
the mystery of Jesus' descent into hell is illuminated as if in
a glaring flash of lightning on a dark night. We must not
forget that these words of the crucified Christ are the opening line of one of Israel's prayers (Ps 22: [21:2]), which sum-
marizes in a shattering way the needs and hopes of this
people chosen by God and apparently at the moment so
utterly abandoned by him. This prayer that rises from the
sheer misery of God's seeming eclipse ends in praises of
God's greatness. This element, too, is present in Jesus' death
cry, which has been recently described by Ernst Käsemann
as a prayer sent up from hell, as the raising of a standard,
the first commandment, in the wilderness of God's apparent absence: "The Son still holds on to faith when faith
seems to have become meaningless and the earthly reality
proclaims absent the God of whom the first thief and the
mocking crowd speak—not for nothing. His cry is not for
life and survival, not for himself, but for the Father. His
cry stands against the reality of the whole world." After
this, do we still need to ask what worship must be in our
hour of darkness? Can it be anything else but the cry from
the depths in company with the Lord who "has descended
into hell" and who has established the nearness of God in
the midst of abandonment by God?

Let us try to investigate another aspect of this complex
mystery, which cannot be elucidated from one side alone.
Let us first take account of one of the findings of exegesis.
We are told that in this article of the Creed, the word "hell"
is only a wrong translation of *sheol* (in Greek, Hades), which
denoted in Hebrew the state after death, which was very

vaguely imagined as a kind of shadow existence, more non-being than being. Accordingly, the statement meant originally, say the scholars, only that Jesus entered *sheol*, that is, that he died. This may be perfectly correct, but the question remains whether it makes the matter any simpler or less mysterious. In my view, it is only at this point that we come face to face with the problem of what death really is, what happens when someone dies, that is, enters into the fate of death. Confronted with this question, we all have to admit our embarrassment. No one really knows the answer because we all live on this side of death and are unfamiliar with the experience of death. But perhaps we can try to begin formulating an answer by starting again from Jesus' cry on the Cross, which we found to contain the heart of what Jesus' descent into hell, his sharing of man's mortal fate, really means. In this last prayer of Jesus, as in the scene on the Mount of Olives, what appears as the innermost heart of his Passion is not any physical pain but radical loneliness, complete abandonment. But in the last analysis what comes to light here is simply the abyss of loneliness of man in general, of man who is alone in his innermost being. This loneliness, which is usually thickly overlaid but is nevertheless the true situation of man, is at the same time in fundamental contradiction with the nature of man, who cannot exist alone; he needs company. That is why loneliness is the region of fear, which is rooted in the exposure of a being that must exist but is pushed out into a situation with which it is impossible for him to deal.

A concrete example may help to make this clearer. When a child has to walk through the woods in the dark, he feels frightened, however convincingly he has been shown that there is no reason at all to be frightened. As soon as he is alone in the darkness, and thus has the experience of utter loneliness, fear arises, the fear peculiar to man, which is not fear of anything in particular but simply fear in itself. Fear of a particular thing is basically harmless; it can be removed by taking away the thing concerned. For example, if someone is afraid of a vicious dog, the matter can be swiftly settled by putting the dog on a chain. Here we come up against something much deeper, namely, the fact that where man falls into extreme loneliness he is not afraid of anything definite that could be explained away; on the contrary, he experiences the fear of loneliness, the uneasiness and vulnerability of his own nature, something that cannot be overcome by rational means. Let us take another example. If someone has to keep watch alone in a room with a dead person, he will always feel his position to be somehow or other eerie, even if he is unwilling to admit it to himself and is capable of explaining to himself rationally the groundlessness of his fear. He knows perfectly well in his own mind that the corpse can do him no harm and that his position might be more dangerous if the person concerned were still alive. What arises here is a completely different kind of fear, not fear of anything in particular, but, in being alone with death, the eerieness of loneliness in itself, the exposed nature of existence.

How then, we must ask, can such fear be overcome if proof of its groundlessness has no effect? Well, the child will lose his fear the moment there is a hand there to take him and lead him and a voice to talk to him; at the moment, therefore, at which he experiences the fellowship of a loving human being. Similarly, he who is alone with the corpse will feel the bout of fear recede when there is a human being with him, when he experiences the nearness of a "you". This conquest of fear reveals at the same time once again the nature of the fear: that it is the fear of loneliness, the anxiety of a being that can only live with a fellow being. The fear peculiar to man cannot be overcome by reason but only by the presence of someone who loves him.

We must examine our question still further. If there were such a thing as a loneliness that could no longer be penetrated and transformed by the word of another; if a state of abandonment were to arise that was so deep that no "you" could reach into it any more, then we should have real, total loneliness and dreadfulness, what theology calls "hell". We can now define exactly what this word means: it denotes a loneliness that the word love can no longer penetrate and that therefore indicates the exposed nature of existence in itself. In this connection, who can fail to remember that writers and philosophers of our time take the view that basically all encounters between human beings remain superficial, that no man has access to the real depths of another? According to this view, no one can really penetrate into the innermost being of someone else; every encounter, beautiful as it may seem, basically only dulls the incurable wound of loneliness. Thus hell, despair, would dwell at the very bottom of our existence, in the shape of that loneliness which is as inescapable as it is dreadful. As is well known, Sartre based his anthropology on this idea. But even such an apparently conciliatory and tranquilly cheerful poet as Hermann Hesse allows the same thought to appear in his work:

> Seltsam, im Nebel zu wandern!
> Leben ist Einsamsein.
> Kein Mensch kennt den andern,
> Jeder ist allein![4]

In truth—one thing is certain: there exists a night into whose solitude no voice reaches; there is a door through which

[4] Curious, to walk in a mist
Life is loneliness.
No man knows his neighbor,
Everyone is alone!

we can only walk alone—the door of death. In the last analysis, all the fear in the world is fear of this loneliness. From this point of view, it is possible to understand why the Old Testament has only one word for hell *and* death, the word *sheol*; it regards them as ultimately identical. Death is absolute loneliness. But the loneliness into which love can no longer advance is—hell.

This brings us back to our starting point, the article of the Creed that speaks of the descent into hell. This article thus asserts that Christ strode through the gate of our final loneliness, that in his Passion he went down into the abyss of our abandonment. Where no voice can reach us any longer, there is he. Hell is thereby overcome, or, to be more accurate, death, which was previously hell, is hell no longer. Neither is the same any longer because there is life in the midst of death, because love dwells in it. Now only deliberate self-enclosure is hell or, as the Bible calls it, the second death (Rev 20:14, for example). But death is no longer the path into icy solitude; the gates of *sheol* have been opened. From this angle, I think, one can understand the images—which at first sight look so mythological—of the Fathers, who speak of fetching up the dead, of the opening of the gates. The apparently mythical passage in Saint Matthew's Gospel becomes comprehensible, too, the passage that says that at the death of Jesus tombs opened and the bodies of the saints were raised (Mt 27:52). The door of death stands open since life—love—has dwelt in death. . . .

2. *"He ascended into heaven"*

To our generation, whose critical faculty has been awakened by Bultmann, talk of the Ascension, together with that of the descent into hell, conjures up that picture of a three-story world which we call mythical and regard as finished with once and for all. "Above" and "below", the world is everywhere just world, governed everywhere by the same physical laws, in principle susceptible everywhere of the same kind of investigation. It has no stories, and the concepts "above" and "below" are relative, depending on the standpoint of the observer. Indeed, since there is no absolute point of reference (and the earth certainly does not represent one), basically one can no longer speak at all of "above" and "below"—or even of "left" and "right"; the cosmos no longer exhibits any fixed directions.

No one today will seriously contest these discoveries. There is no longer such a thing as a world arranged literally in three stories. But was such a conception ever really intended in the articles of faith about the Lord's descent into hell and Ascension to heaven? It certainly provided the imagery for them, but it was just as certainly not the decisive factual element in them. On the contrary, the two tenets, together with faith in the historical Jesus, express the total range of human existence, which certainly spans three metaphysical dimensions if not three cosmic stories. To that extent it is only logical that the attitude that at the moment is considered "modern" should dispense not only with the Ascension and the descent into hell but also with the historical Jesus, that is, with all three dimensions of human existence; what is left *can* only be a variously draped ghost, on which—understandably—no one any longer wishes to build anything serious.

But what do our three dimensions really imply? We have already come to see that the descent into hell does not really refer to any outer depths of the cosmos; these are quite unnecessary to it. In the basic text, the prayer of the crucified Christ to the God who has abandoned him, there is no trace of any cosmic reference. On the contrary, this article of the Creed turns our gaze to the depths of human existence, which reach down into the valley of death, into the zone of untouchable loneliness and rejected love, and thus embrace the dimension of hell, carrying it within themselves as one of their own possibilities. Hell, existence in the definitive rejection of "being for", is not a cosmographical destination but a dimension of human nature, the abyss into which it reaches down at its lower end. We know today better than ever before that everyone's existence touches these depths; and since in the last analysis mankind is "*one* man", these depths affect not only the individual but also the one body of the whole human race, which must therefore bear the burden of them as a corporate whole. From this angle it can be understood once again how Christ, the "new Adam", undertook to bear the burden of these depths with us and did not wish to remain sublimely unaffected by them; conversely, of course, total rejection in all its unfathomability has only now become possible.

On the other hand, the Ascension of Christ points to the opposite end of human existence, which stretches out an infinite distance above and below itself. This existence embraces, as the opposite pole to utter solitude, to the untouchability of rejected love, the possibility of contact with all other men through the medium of contact with the divine love itself, so that human existence can find its geometrical place, so to speak, inside God's own being. The two possibilities of man thus brought to mind by the words heaven and hell are, it is true, completely different in nature and can be quite clearly distinguished from each other. The depths we call hell man can only give to himself. Indeed, we must put it more pointedly: Hell consists in man's being unwilling to receive anything, in his desire to be self-sufficient. It is the expression of enclosure in one's own being alone. These depths accordingly consist by nature of just this: that man will not accept, will not take anything, but wants to stand entirely on his own feet, to be sufficient unto himself. If this becomes utterly radical, then man has become the untouchable, the solitary, the reject. Hell is wanting only to be oneself; what happens when man barricades himself up in himself. Conversely, it is the nature of that upper end of the scale which we have called heaven that it can only be received, just as one can only give hell to oneself. "Heaven" is by nature what one has not made oneself and cannot make oneself; in Scholastic language it was said to be, as grace, a *donum indebitum et superadditum naturae* (an unowed gift added over and above nature). As fulfilled love, heaven can always only be granted to man; but hell is the loneliness of the man who will not accept it, who declines the status of beggar and withdraws into himself.

Only from this standpoint does it become clear now what is really meant in the Christian view by heaven. It is not to be understood as an everlasting place above the world or simply as an eternal metaphysical region. On the contrary, "heaven" and "the Ascension of Christ" are indivisibly connected; it is only this connection that makes clear the christological, personal, history-centered meaning of the Christian tidings of heaven. Let us look at it from another angle: heaven is not a place that, before Christ's Ascension, was barred off by a positive, punitive decree of God's, to be opened up one day in just as positive a way. On the contrary, the reality of heaven only comes into existence through the confluence of God and man. Heaven is to be defined as the contact of the being "man" with the being "God"; this confluence of God and man took place once and for all in Christ when he went beyond bios through death to new life. Heaven is accordingly that future of man and of mankind which the latter cannot give to itself, which is therefore closed to it so long as it waits for itself, and which was first and fundamentally opened up in the man whose field of existence was God and through whom God entered into the creature "man".

Therefore heaven is always more than a private, individual destiny; it is necessarily connected with the "last Adam", with the definitive man, and, accordingly, with the future of man as a whole.

3. "Resurrection of the body"

The content of the New Testament hope of resurrection[5]

The article about the resurrection of the body puts us in a curious dilemma. We have discovered anew the indivisibility of man; we live our corporality with a new intensity and experience it as the indispensable way of realizing the one being of man. From this angle we can understand afresh the biblical message, which promises immortality, not to a separated soul, but to the whole man. Such feelings have in this century made Lutheran theology in particular turn emphatically against the Greek doctrine of the immortality of the soul, which is wrongly regarded as a Christian idea, too. In reality, so it is said, this idea expresses a thoroughly un-Christian dualism; the Christian faith knows only of the waking of the dead by God's power. But doubts arise at once here: The Greek doctrine of immortality may well be problematical, but is not the biblical testimony still more incapable of fulfillment for us? The unity of man, fine, but who can imagine, on the basis of our present-day image of the world, a resurrection of the body? This resurrection would also imply—or so it seems, at any rate—a new heaven

[5] The following arguments are closely linked to those in my article "Auferstehung" in *Sacramentum Mundi*, ed. Rahner and Darlap, 1:397–402 (Freiburg, 1967), 397–402, where there is also a bibliography.

and a new earth; it would require immortal bodies needing no sustenance and a completely different condition of matter. But is this not all completely absurd, quite contrary to our understanding of matter and its modes of behavior, and therefore hopelessly mythological?

Well, I think that in fact one can only arrive at an answer if one inquires carefully into the real intentions of the biblical testimony and at the same time considers anew the relation between the biblical and the Greek ideas. For their encounter with each other has modified both conceptions and thus overlaid the original intentions of both approaches with a new combined view that we must first remove if we want to find our way back to the beginning. First of all, the hope for the resurrection of the dead simply represents the basic form of the biblical hope for immortality; it appears in the New Testament, not really as a supplement to a preceding and independent immortality of the soul, but as the fundamental statement on the fate of man. There were, it is true, in late Jewish teachings hints of immortality on the Greek pattern, and this was probably one of the reasons why very soon the all-embracing scope of the idea of resurrection in the Graeco-Roman world was no longer grasped. Instead, the Greek notion of the immortality of the soul and the biblical message of the resurrection of the dead were each understood as half the answer to the question of the fate of man, and the two were added together. It was thought that, to the already existing Greek foreknowledge about the immortality of the soul, the Bible added the revelation that at the end of the world bodies would be awakened, too, to share henceforth forever the fate of the soul—damnation or bliss.

As opposed to this, we must grasp the fact that originally it was not a question of two complementary ideas; on the contrary, we are confronted with two different outlooks, which cannot simply be added together: the image of man, of God, and of the future is in each case quite different, and thus at bottom each of the two views can only be understood as an attempt at a total answer to the question of human fate. The Greek conception is based on the idea that man is composed of two mutually foreign substances, one of which (the body) perishes, while the other (the soul) is in itself imperishable and therefore goes on existing in its own right independent of any other beings. Indeed, it was only in the separation from the body, which is essentially foreign to it, so they thought, that the soul came fully into its own. The biblical train of thought, on the other hand, presupposes the undivided unity of man; for example, Scripture contains no word denoting only the body (separated and distinguished from the soul), while conversely in the vast majority of cases the word soul, too, means the whole corporeally existing man; the few places where a different view can be discerned hover to a certain extent between Greek and Hebrew thinking and in any case by no means abandon the old view. The awakening of the dead (not of bodies!) of which Scripture speaks is thus concerned with the salvation of the *one*, undivided man, not just with the fate of one (perhaps secondary) half of man. It now also becomes clear that the real heart of the faith in resurrection does not consist at all in the idea of the restoration of bodies, to which we have reduced it in our thinking; such is the case even though this is the pictorial image used throughout the Bible. What, then, is the real content of the hope symbolically proclaimed in the Bible in the shape of the resurrection of the dead? I think that this can best be worked out by means of a comparison with the dualistic conception of ancient philosophy.

1. The idea of immortality denoted in the Bible by the word "resurrection" is an immortality of the "person", of

the *one* creation "man". Whereas in Greek thought the typical man is a perishable creature, which as such does not live on but goes two different ways in accordance with its heterogeneous formation out of body and soul, according to the biblical belief it is precisely this being, man, that as such goes on existing, even if transformed.

2. It is a question of a "dialogic" immortality (=awakening!); that is, immortality results, not simply from the self-evident inability of the indivisible to die, but from the saving deed of the lover who has the necessary power: man can no longer totally perish because he is known and loved by God. All love wants eternity, and God's love not only wants it but effects it and is it. In fact, the biblical idea of awakening grew directly out of this dialogical theme: he who prays knows in faith that God will restore the right (Job 19:25ff.; Ps 73:23ff.); faith is convinced that those who have suffered in the interests of God will also receive a share in the redemption of the promise (2 Macc 7:9ff.). Immortality as conceived by the Bible proceeds, not from the intrinsic power of what is in itself indestructible, but from being drawn into the dialogue with the Creator; *that is why* it must be called awakening. Because the Creator intends, not just the soul, but the man physically existing in the midst of history and gives *him* immortality, it must be called "awakening of the dead" = "of men". It should be noted here that even in the formula of the Creed, which speaks of the "resurrection of the body", the word "body" means in effect "the world of man" (in the sense of biblical expressions like "all flesh will see God's salvation", and so on); even here the word is not meant in the sense of a corporality isolated from the soul.

3. That the awakening is expected on the "Last Day", at the end of history, and in the company of all mankind

indicates the communal character of human immortality, which is related to the whole of mankind, from which, toward which, and with which the individual has lived and hence finds salvation or loses it. At bottom this association results automatically from the collective character of the biblical idea of immortality. To the soul as conceived by the Greeks, the body, and so history, too, is completely exterior; the soul goes on existing apart from them and needs no other being in order to do so. For man understood as a unity, on the other hand, fellowship with his fellowmen is constitutive; if he is to live on, then this dimension cannot be excluded. Thus, on the biblical premise, the much-discussed question of whether after death there can be any fellowship between men seems to be solved; at bottom it could only arise at all through a preponderance of the Greek element in the intellectual premises: where the "communion of saints" is an article of faith, the idea of the *anima separata* (the "separated soul" of Scholastic theology) has in the last analysis become obsolete.

The full elaboration of these ideas became possible only after the New Testament had given concrete shape to the biblical hope—the Old Testament by itself ultimately leaves the question about the future of man in the air. Only with Christ, the man who is "one with the Father", the man through whom the being "man" has entered into God's eternity, does the future of man definitely appear open. Only in him, the "second Adam", is the question of man's identity finally answered. Christ is man, completely; to that extent the question of who we men are is present in him. But he is at the same time God speaking to us, the "Word of God". In him the conversation between God and man that has been going on since the beginning of history has entered a new phase: in him the Word of God became "flesh" and really gained admission into our existence. But if the dialogue of God with man means life, if it is true that God's partner in the dialogue himself has life precisely through being addressed by him who lives forever, then this means that Christ, as God's Word to us, is himself "the resurrection and the life" (Jn 11:25). It also means that the entry into Christ known as faith becomes in a qualified sense an entry into that being known and loved by God which is immortality: "Whoever believes in the Son *has* eternal life" (see Jn 3:15; 3:36; 5:24). Only from this angle is it possible to understand the train of thought of the fourth evangelist, who in his account of the Lazarus episode wants to make the reader understand that resurrection is not just a distant happening at the end of the world but happens now through faith. Whoever believes is in the conversation with God that is life and that outlasts death. At this point, too, the "dialogic" strand in the biblical concept of immortality, the one related directly to God, and the "human fellowship" strand meet and join. For in Christ, the man, we meet God; but in him we also meet the community of those others whose path to God runs through him and so toward one another. The orientation toward God is in him at the same time toward the community of mankind, and only the acceptance of this community is movement toward God, who does not exist apart from Christ and thus not apart either from the context of the whole history of humanity and its common task.

This also clarifies the question, much discussed in the patristic period and again since Luther, of the "intermediate state" between death and resurrection: the existence with Christ inaugurated by faith is the start of resurrected life and, therefore, outlasts death (see Phil 1:23; 2 Cor 5:8; 1 Thess 5:10). The dialogue of faith is itself already life, which can no longer be shattered by death. The idea of the sleep

of death that has been continually discussed by Lutheran
theologians and recently also brought into play by the Dutch
Catechism is therefore untenable on the evidence of the
New Testament and not even justifiable by the frequent
occurrence in the New Testament of the word "sleep": the
whole train of thought of every book in the New Testament is completely at variance with such an interpretation,
which could hardly be inferred even from late Jewish thinking about the life after death.

The essential immortality of man

The foregoing reflections may have clarified to some extent
what is involved in the biblical pronouncements about the
resurrection: their essential content is not the conception of
a restoration of bodies to souls after a long interval; their
aim is to tell men that they, they themselves, live on; not by
virtue of their own power, but because they are known and
loved by God in such a way that they can no longer perish.
In contrast to the dualistic conception of immortality expressed
in the Greek body-soul schema, the biblical formula of immortality through awakening means to convey a collective and
dialogic conception of immortality: the essential part of man,
the person, remains; that which has ripened in the course of
this earthly existence of corporeal spirituality and spiritual-
ized corporeality goes on existing in a different fashion. It
goes on existing because it lives in God's memory. And because
it is the man himself who will live, not an isolated soul, the
element of human fellowship is also part of the future; for
this reason the future of the individual man will only then
be full when the future of humanity is fulfilled.

A whole series of questions arises at this point. The first
is this: Does this view not make immortality into a pure
grace, although in reality it must fall to man's lot by virtue

of his nature as man? In other words, does one not finish up here with an immortality only for the pious and, thus, in a division of human fate that is unacceptable? To put it in theological terms, are we not here confusing the natural immortality of the being "man" with the supernatural gift of eternal love that makes man happy? Must we not hold fast, precisely for the sake of the humanity of the Christian faith, to natural immortality, for the reason that a continued existence conceived in purely christological terms would necessarily slide into the miraculous and mythological? This last question can indubitably be answered only in the affirmative. But this is by no means at variance with our original premise. It, too, entitled us to say decisively: The immortality that, precisely because of its dialogic character, we have called "awakening" falls to the lot of man, *every* man, as man, and is not some secondary "supernatural" addition. But we must then go on to ask: What really makes man into man? What is the definitive distinguishing mark of man? To that we shall have to answer: The distinguishing mark of man, seen from above, is his being addressed by God, the fact that he is God's partner in a dialogue, the being called by God. Seen from below, this means that man is the being who can think of God, the being opened onto transcendence. The point here is not whether he really does think of God, really does open himself to him, but that he is in principle the being who is in himself capable of doing so, even if in fact, for whatever reasons, he is perhaps never able to utilize this capacity.

Now one could say: Is it not, then, much simpler to see the distinguishing mark of man in the fact that he has a spiritual, immortal soul? This definition is perfectly sound; but we are in fact at this moment engaged in the process of trying to elucidate its concrete meaning. The two definitions are not in the least contradictory; they simply express the same thing in different modes of thought. For "having a spiritual soul" means precisely being willed, known, and loved by God in a special way; it means being a creature called by God to an eternal dialogue and, therefore, capable for its own part of knowing God and of replying to him. What we call in substantialist language "having a soul" we will describe in a more historical, actual language as "being God's partner in a dialogue". This does not mean that talk of the soul is false (as is sometimes asserted today by a one-sided and uncritical biblical approach); in one respect it is, indeed, even necessary in order to describe the whole of what is involved here. But, on the other hand, it also needs to be complemented if we are not to fall back into a dualistic conception that cannot do justice to the dialogic and personalistic view of the Bible.

So when we say that man's immortality is based on his dialogic relationship with and reliance upon God, whose love alone bestows eternity, we are not claiming a special destiny for the pious but emphasizing the essential immortality of man as man. After the foregoing reflections, it is also perfectly possible to develop the idea out of the body-soul schema, whose importance, perhaps even indispensability, lies in the fact that it emphasizes this essential character of human immortality. But it must also be continually put back in the biblical perspective and corrected by it in order to remain serviceable to the view of man's future opened up by faith. For the rest, it becomes evident once again at this point that in the last analysis one cannot make a neat distinction between "natural" and "supernatural": the basic dialogue that first makes man into man makes a smooth transition into the dialogue of grace known as Jesus Christ. How could it be otherwise if Christ actually is the "second Adam", the real fulfillment of that infinite longing which arises from the first Adam—from man in general?

Christ the Liberator

"Seek the Things That Are Above"
(Colossians 3:1)

"This is the day the Lord has made, let us rejoice and be glad in it": thus we sing in the words of one of the psalms of Israel, a psalm that had been waiting, in a manner of speaking, for the risen Lord and so became the Easter hymn of Christians. We sing the Alleluia, a Hebrew word that has become a timeless expression of the joy of the redeemed.

But are we right to be glad? Or is joy not almost a kind of cynicism, a kind of mockery, in a world that is so full of suffering? Are we redeemed? Is the world redeemed?

The shots that murdered the Archbishop of San Salvador during the Consecration of the Mass are nothing more than a harsh searchlight showing up the violence, the human barbarization, that has been unleashed all over the earth. In Cambodia an entire people is being slowly wiped out—and no one wants to know.[1] And everywhere we find that people are suffering for their faith, their convictions; their rights are being trampled on. Recently the Russian priest Dmitri Dudko, no doubt sensing that he would shortly be

---

Translated by Graham Harrison.

[1] This was written in 1985, when many had been or were being killed by the Khmer Rouge and the Vietnamese.—Ed.

arrested, issued a message to all Christians, in which he says he is speaking from Golgotha, which is also the place where the risen Lord appeared to the disciples behind locked doors. He sees Moscow as Golgotha, where the Lord was crucified, but he sees it also as the place where the risen Lord becomes present and shows himself, in spite of (or even because of) the locked doors intended to keep him out.

Looking at the world, we may well wonder whether we actually have time to think of God and divine things, or whether we should not rather apply all our energies to improving the lot of people on earth. This was the attitude of Bertolt Brecht when he wrote:

> Do not delude yourselves with lies,
> Like the beasts man simply dies,
> and after that comes nothing.

He regarded belief in a world beyond, in the resurrection, as a deception that hinders man from fully laying hold of this world, of life. But if we stress man's similarity to the animals and oppose this to his likeness to God, we shall very soon regard man simply as an animal. And if, as another modern poet has said, we die like dogs, we shall very soon live like dogs, too, treating one another like dogs or rather as no dog should ever be treated.

The Jewish philosopher Theodor Adorno had a more profound view of things. In the passionate, messianic yearning of his people, he continually asked how a just world, how justice in the world, could be created. Ultimately he arrived at this insight: If there is to be real justice in the world, it must be for all and for all time, and that means justice for the dead as well. It would have to be a justice that retroactively heals all past suffering. And this would imply the resurrection of the dead.

Against this background I think we can hear the message of Easter in a new way. Christ is risen! There is justice for the world! There is complete justice for all, which is able retroactively to make good all past sufferings, and this is because God exists, and he has the power to do it. As Saint Bernard of Clairvaux once put it, although God cannot suffer, he can be compassionate. And he can be compassionate because he can love. It is this power of compassion, springing from the power of love, which is able to make good the past and create justice. Christ is risen: this means that there is a power that is able to create justice and that is actively creating it. That is why the message of the Resurrection is not only a hymn to God but a hymn to the power of his love and hence a hymn to man, to the earth, and to matter. The whole is saved. God does not allow any part of his creation to sink silently into a past that has gone forever. He has created everything so that it should exist, as the Book of Wisdom says. He has created everything so that all should be one and should belong to him, so that "God shall be all in all."

The question arises however: How can we respond and live up to these Resurrection tidings? How can this message come into our midst and become reality? For Easter is, as it were, the brilliance of the open door that leads out of the injustice of the world as well as the challenge to follow this radiant light and to show it to others, knowing that it is not a deluding dream but the real light, the genuine way out. But how can we get there? The answer is given in the Easter Sunday reading in which Paul writes to the Colossians: Christ is risen. Seek the things that are above, where Christ is. Set your minds on things that are above, not on things that are on earth (Col 3:1f.).

Listening with today's ears to Saint Paul's exhortation to embrace the Easter message, the Easter reality, we are probably tempted to say, "So it is an escape into heaven after all; it is a flight from the world." But this is a crude misunderstanding. For it is a basic law of human life that only the one who loses himself finds himself. It is the person who tries to hold on to himself, unwilling to go beyond himself, who fails to find his own self. The man who wants to possess himself and does not give himself will not receive himself as gift. This fundamental law of human nature, which springs from the fundamental law of the love of the Trinity, from the very nature of the being of God (who, in giving himself in the form of love, is the true reality and the true power), applies to the whole realm of our relationship to reality.

It is precisely the person who desires only matter who dishonors it, robbing it of its greatness and dignity. The Christian honors matter more than the materialist does by opening it up in such a way that, here too, God may be all in all. The person who seeks only the body diminishes it. Desiring only the things of this world, he actually destroys the earth. We minister to the earth by transcending it. We heal it by not leaving it alone, by not remaining isolated ourselves. Just as the earth physically needs the sun in order to remain a life-bearing planet, and just as it needs the coherence of the universe in order to travel its path, so too the spiritual cosmos of man's earth needs the light from above, the integrating power enabling it to open itself up. We must not close the earth in upon itself if we are to save it; we must not cling to it greedily. We must throw open its doors so that the true energies by which it lives and that are so necessary to us can be present in it. Seek the things that are above! This is the earth's task: to live with a view to the world above, to live toward the heights, toward what is lofty and great, to resist the gravitational pull from below, the forces of disintegration. It means following the Risen One, ministering to justice, to the salvation of this world.

The first message of the risen Lord, communicated to those who were his by means of the angels and the women, is: Come, follow me; I am going before you! Resurrection-faith is a stepping forward along the way. It can be nothing else than a following in the steps of Christ, a discipleship of Christ. In his Easter gospel, John has expressed very clearly where and how Christ has gone and whither we are to follow him: "I am ascending to my Father and your Father, to my God and your God" (Jn 20:17). He tells Magdalen that she cannot touch him now but only when he has ascended. We cannot touch him in such a way as to bring him back into this world, but we can touch him by following him, by ascending with him. That is why Christian tradition deliberately speaks not simply of following Jesus but of following Christ. We follow, not a dead man, but the living Christ. We are not trying to imitate a life that is past and gone or to turn it into a program for action with all kinds of compromises and revaluations. We must not rob discipleship of what is essential to it, namely, Cross and Resurrection and Christ's divine Sonship, his being "with the Father". These things are fundamental. Discipleship means that now we can go where (again according to John) Peter and the Jews initially could not go. But now that he has gone before us, we can go there, too. Discipleship means accepting the entire path, going forward into those things that are above, the hidden things that are the real ones: truth, love, our being children of God. Discipleship of this kind happens only, however, in the modality of the Cross, in the true losing of self that alone can open the treasury of God and of the earth, that alone releases, as it were, the living wellsprings of the depths and causes the power of real life to stream into this world. Discipleship is a stepping-forward into what is hidden in order to find, through this genuine loss of self, what it is to be a human being. It also means discovering that store of joy of which the world stands in such urgent need. Not only do we have a right, we also have a duty to rejoice, because the Lord has given us joy and the world is waiting for it.

Here is an illustration from recent times. The British doctor Sheila Cassidy (who in 1978 entered the Benedictine Order) was imprisoned and tortured in Chile in 1975 for having given medical treatment to a revolutionary. Shortly after being tortured, she was transferred to another cell, where she found a tattered Bible. She opened it, and the first thing she saw was a picture of a man prostrate under lightning, thunder, and hail. Immediately she identified herself with this man, saw herself in him. Then she looked farther and saw in the upper part of the picture a mighty hand, the hand of God, and the text from the eighth chapter of the Letter to the Romans, a text that comes straight from the center of Resurrection-faith: "Nothing can separate us from the love of Christ" (8:39). And whereas at first it was the bottom half of the picture she experienced, her being invaded by all that was terrible, crushing her like a helpless worm, she gradually came to experience more and more the other part of the picture, the powerful hand and the "Nothing can separate us".

At first she still prayed, "Lord, let me out of here", but this interior shaking of the prison bars turned more and more into that truly free composure which prays, with Jesus Christ: "Not my will, but yours, be done." Furthermore, she discovered that, as a result, she was filled with a great freedom and kindness toward those who hated her; now she could love them, for she saw their hatred as their distress and imprisonment. Subsequently she was put together with Marxist women; she held services for them, and they too discovered this liberation from hatred and the great freedom that sprang from it. She says: "We knew that this freedom we had behind strong walls was not imagination; it was a quite tangible reality." After eight weeks she was released. What stayed with her, however, was that now she continually found Christ in everyday life, in people, and in things. Thus she came to understand Chesterton when he described men who, signed with Christ's Cross, cheerfully walk through darkness. Finding this hidden life means releasing the sources of this world's energy, linking the world to the power that can save it, giving it the resources for which it seeks in vain within itself. It means digging for and uncovering the wellspring of joy that can save and transform things and people and that has the power to undo and make good past suffering. Seek the things that are above! This is not a mere clutching at a straw but a setting-out on the great Easter journey into the region of genuine reality.[2]

Recently I was deeply disturbed to read, in the words of an Indian woman missionary, that we are simply not in any position to show Christ to Indians, because most missionaries, totally taken up with exterior activity, are by Indian standards not really able to pray. This inability means that they in no way touch the point of the inner oneness of God and man; thus it is impossible for them to show the world the mystery of the Incarnate One and to lead the world to the freedom that comes from that mystery. This, then, is the first challenge of Easter: we are summoned to begin the journey inward and upward, toward the hidden, true reality, and we must find that it is reality. We can have faith in the Risen One only if we have encountered him. We can encounter him only by following him. Only if both things are true of us can we bear witness to him and carry his light into this world.

<hr />

[2] Cf. S. Cassidy, "Beten in Bedrängnis: Gebetserfahrungen in der Haft in Chile", *Geist und Leben* 53 (1980): 81–91.

One of the psalms of Israel, which the Church understands as a psalm of the Passion of Jesus Christ and which
she long prayed at the beginning of every Mass, is this:
"Give me justice, O God." It is the cry of a world in the
midst of suffering. Give me justice, O God! And he has
said Yes. Christ is risen! What was past and beyond recall
has been recalled. The power of transformation is available
to us. Let our lives be one whole movement toward it! Let
us seek the things that are above!

To Judge the Living and the Dead

He Will Come Again

Rudolf Bultmann reckons that the belief in an "end of the world" signaled by the return of the Lord in judgment is one of those ideas, like the Lord's descent into hell and Ascension into heaven, which for modern man are "disposed of". Every reasonable person, he declares, is convinced that the world will go on as it has done now for nearly two thousand years since the eschatological proclamation of the New Testament. It seems all the more important to clarify our thinking on this point since the biblical treatment of it unquestionably contains marked cosmological elements and therefore reaches into the domain that we view as the field of natural science. Of course, in the phrase about the end of the world, the word "world" does not mean primarily the physical structure of the cosmos but the world of man, human history; thus in the first instance this manner of speaking means that *this* kind of world—the human world—will come to an end that is dictated and achieved by God. But it cannot be denied that the Bible presents this essentially anthropological event in cosmological (and also partly in political) imagery. How

Translated by J.R. Foster.

far it is a question *only* of imagery and how close the imagery is to the reality is difficult to determine.

Certainly one can only base one's observations on this subject on the larger context of the Bible's whole view of the world. And for the Bible the cosmos and man are not two clearly separable quantities, with the cosmos forming the fortuitous scene of human existence, which in itself could be parted from the cosmos and allowed to accomplish itself without a world. On the contrary, world and human existence belong necessarily to one another, so that neither a worldless man nor even a world without man seems thinkable. The first of these two concepts can be accepted again today without argument; and after what we have learned from Teilhard, the second should no longer be entirely incomprehensible, either. Going on from there, one might be tempted to say that the biblical message about the end of the world and the return of the Lord is not simply anthropology in cosmic imagery; that it does not even merely present a cosmological aspect alongside an anthropological one but depicts with the inner logic of the total biblical view the coincidence of anthropology and cosmology in definitive Christology and, precisely *therein*, portrays the end of the "world", which in its two-in-one construction out of cosmos and man has always pointed to this unity as its final goal. Cosmos and man, which already belong to each other even though they so often stand opposed to one another, become one through their "complexification" in the larger entity of the love that, as we said earlier, goes beyond and encompasses *bios*. Thus it becomes evident here once again how very much end-eschatology and the breakthrough represented by Jesus' Resurrection are in reality one and the same thing; it becomes clear once again that the New Testament rightly depicts this Resurrection as *the* eschatological happening.

In order to make any further progress we must elaborate this thought a little more clearly. We said just now that the cosmos was not just an outward framework of human history, not a static mold—a kind of container holding all kinds of living creatures that could just as well be poured into a different container. This means, stated positively, that the cosmos is movement; that it is not just a case of history *existing in* it, that the cosmos itself *is* history. It does not merely form the scene of human history; before human history began and later with it, cosmos is itself "history". Finally, there is only one single all-embracing world history, which for all the ups and downs, all the advances and setbacks that it exhibits, nevertheless has a general direction and goes "forward". Of course, to him who only sees a section of it, this piece, even though it may be relatively big, looks like a circling in the same spot. No direction is perceptible. It is only observed by him who begins to see the whole. But in this cosmic movement, as we have already seen, spirit is not just some chance by-product of development, of no importance to the whole; on the contrary, we were able to establish that, in this movement or process, matter and its evolution form the prehistory of spirit or mind.

From this perspective the belief in the second coming of Jesus Christ and in the consummation of the world in that event could be explained as the conviction that our history is advancing to an "omega" point, at which it will become finally and unmistakably clear that the element of stability that seems to us to be the supporting ground of reality, so to speak, is not mere unconscious matter; that, on the contrary, the real, firm ground is mind. Mind holds being together, gives it reality, indeed *is* reality: it is not from below but from above that being receives its capacity to subsist. That there is such a thing as this process of "complexification" of material being through spirit, and from the latter its concentration into a new kind of unity, can already be seen today in a certain sense in the remodeling of the world through technology. In reality's susceptibility to manipulation, the boundaries between nature and technology are already beginning to disappear; we can no longer clearly distinguish one from the other. To be sure, this analogy must be regarded as questionable in more than one respect. Yet such processes hint at a kind of world in which spirit and nature do not simply stand alongside each other but in which spirit, in a new "complexification", draws what apparently is merely natural into itself, thereby creating a new world that at the same time necessarily means the end of the old one. Now the "end of the world" in which the Christian believes is certainly something quite different from the total victory of technology. But the welding together of nature and spirit that occurs in it enables us to grasp in a new way how the reality of belief in the return of Christ is to be conceived: as faith in the final unification of reality by spirit or mind.

This opens the way to a further step. We said before that nature and mind form one single history, which advances in such a way that mind emerges more and more clearly as the all-embracing element and, thus, anthropology and cosmology finally in actual fact coalesce. But this assertion of the increasing "complexification" of the world through mind necessarily implies its unification around a personal center, for mind is not just an undefined something or other; where it exists in its own specific nature, it subsists as individuality, as person. It is true that there is such a thing as "objective mind", mind invested in machines, in works of the most varied kind; but in all these cases mind does not exist in its original, specific form; "objective mind" is always derived from subjective mind; it points back to person, mind's only real mode of existence. Thus the assertion that the world is moving toward a "complexification" through mind also implies that the cosmos is moving toward a unification in the personal.

This confirms once again the infinite precedence of the individual over the universal. This principle, which we developed earlier, appears again here in all its importance. The world is in motion toward unity in the person. The whole draws its meaning from the individual, not the other way about. To appreciate this is also to justify once again Christology's apparent positivism, the conviction—a scandal to men of all periods—that makes one individual the center of history and of the whole. The intrinsic necessity of this "positivism" is thus demonstrated anew: if it is true that at the end stands the triumph of spirit, that is, the triumph of truth, freedom, and love, then it is not just some force or other that finally ends up victorious; what stands at the end is a countenance. The omega of the world is a "you", a person, an individual. The all-encompassing "complexification", the unification infinitely embracing all, is at the same time the final denial of all collectivism, the denial of the fanaticism of the mere idea, even the so-called "idea of Christianity". Man, the person, always takes precedence over the mere idea.

This implies a further and very important consequence. If the breakthrough to the ultra-complexity of the final phase is based on spirit and freedom, then it is by no means a neutral, cosmic drift; it includes responsibility. It does not happen of its own accord, like a physical process, but is based on decisions. That is why the second coming of the Lord is not only salvation, not only the omega that sets everything right, but also judgment. Indeed, at this stage we can actually define the meaning of the talk of judgment. It means precisely this, that the final stage of the world is not the result of a natural current but the result of responsibility that is grounded in freedom. This must also be regarded as the key to understanding why the New Testament clings fast, in spite of its message of grace, to the assertion that at the end men are judged "by their works" and that no one can escape giving account of the way he has lived his life. There is a freedom that is not cancelled out even by grace and, indeed, is brought by it face to face with itself: man's final fate is not forced upon him regardless of the decisions he has made in his life. This assertion is in any case also necessary in order to draw the line between faith and false dogmatism or a false Christian self-confidence. This line alone confirms the equality of men by confirming the identity of their responsibility. Since the days of the early Church Fathers, it has always been an essential task of Christian preaching to make people aware of this identity of responsibility and to contrast it with the false confidence engendered by merely saying, "Lord, Lord!"

It might be useful in this context to recall certain things said by the great Jewish theologian Leo Baeck. The Christian will not entirely agree with them, but he cannot disregard their seriousness. Baeck points to the fact that Israel's "life apart" turned into an awareness of serving the future of mankind. "The *special character of the call* is asserted, but *no exclusiveness of salvation* is proclaimed. Judaism was preserved from falling into the religious narrowness of the concept of a Church that alone confers salvation. Where it is not faith but the deed that leads to God, where the community offers to its children as a sign of spiritual membership the ideal and the task, a place in the covenant of faith cannot of itself guarantee the salvation of the soul." Baeck then shows how this universalism of the salvation founded on the deed crystallizes more and more firmly in the Jewish tradition and finally emerges quite clearly in the "classical" saying: "Even the pious who are not Israelites share

in the eternal bliss." No one will be able to read without
dismay when Baeck then goes on to say that one need only
"compare with this principle Dante's picture of the place of
damnation, the destination of even the best pagans, with all
its cruel images corresponding to the notions entertained
by the Church in the centuries before and after, to feel the
sharpness of the contrast." [1]

Of course, much in this passage is inaccurate and pro-
vokes a counterassertion; nevertheless, it contains a serious
statement. It can make clear in its fashion wherein the indispensability of the article about the universal judgment of all
men "according to their works" lies. It is not part of our
task to consider in detail how this assertion can coexist with
the full weight of the doctrine of grace. Perhaps in the last
analysis it is impossible to escape a paradox whose logic is
completely disclosed only to the experience of a life based
on faith. Anyone who entrusts himself to faith becomes
aware that both exist: the radical character of the grace that
frees helpless man and, no less, the abiding seriousness of
the responsibility that summons man day after day. Both
together mean that the Christian enjoys, on the one hand,
the liberating, detached tranquility of him who lives on that
excess of divine justice known as Jesus Christ. There is a
tranquility that knows: in the last analysis, I cannot destroy
what *he* has built up. For in himself man lives with the
dreadful knowledge that his power to destroy is infinitely
greater than his power to build up. But this same man knows
that in Christ the power to build up has proved infinitely
stronger. This is the source of a profound freedom, a knowledge of God's unrepentant love; he sees through all our
errors and remains well disposed to us. It becomes possible
to do one's own work fearlessly; it has shed its sinister aspect

[1] L. Baeck, *Das Wesen des Judentums*, 6th ed. (Cologne, 1960), 69.

because it has lost its power to destroy: the issue of the world does not depend on us but is in God's hands. At the same time the Christian knows, however, that he is not free to do whatever he pleases, that his activity is not a game that God allows him and does not take seriously. He knows that he must answer for his actions, that he owes an account as a steward of what has been entrusted to him. There can only be responsibility where there is someone to be responsible to, someone to put the questions. Faith in the Last Judgment holds this questioning of our life over our heads so that we cannot forget it for a moment. Nothing and no one empowers us to trivialize the tremendous seriousness involved in such knowledge; it shows our life to be a serious business and precisely by doing so gives it its dignity.

"To judge the living and the dead"—this also means that no one but *he* has the right to judge in the end. This implies that the unrighteousness of the world does not have the last word, not even by being wiped out indiscriminately in a universal act of grace; on the contrary, there is a last court of appeal that preserves justice in order thus to be able to perfect love. A love that overthrew justice would create injustice and thus cease to be anything but a caricature of love. True love is excess of justice, excess that goes farther than justice, but never destruction of justice, which must be and must remain the basic form of love.

Of course, one must guard against the opposite extreme. It cannot be denied that belief in the Last Judgment has at times assumed in the Christian consciousness a form in which, in practice, it was bound to lead to the destruction of the full faith in the redemption and the promise of mercy. The example always adduced is the profound contrast between *Maran atha* and *Dies irae*. The early Christians, with their cry "Our Lord, come" (*Maran atha*), interpreted the second coming of Jesus as an event full of hope and joy, stretching their arms out longingly toward it as the moment of the great fulfillment. To the Christians of the Middle Ages, on the other hand, that moment appeared as the terrifying "day of wrath" (*Dies irae*), which makes man feel like dying of woe and terror and to which he looks forward with fear and dread. The return of Christ is then only judgment, the day of the great reckoning that threatens everyone. Such a view forgets a decisive aspect of Christianity, which is thus reduced for all practical purposes to moralism and robbed of that hope and joy which are the very breath of its life.

Perhaps it will have to be admitted that the tendency to such a false development, which sees only the dangers of responsibility and no longer the freedom of love, is already present in the Creed, in which the idea of Christ's second coming is reduced, at any rate verbally, to the idea of judgment: "He will come again to judge the living and the dead." Of course, in the circles that formed the spiritual home of the Creed, the original Christian tradition was still very much alive; the phrase about the Last Judgment was taken in self-evident conjunction with the message of mercy. The statement that it is *Jesus* who judges immediately tinged the judgment with hope. I should just like to quote a passage from the so-called *Second Epistle of Clement* in which this becomes quite clear: "Brothers, we must think of Jesus as God, as he who judges the living and the dead. We must not think little of our salvation, for by thinking little of him we also think little of our hope." [2]

Here the real emphasis of this article of the Creed becomes evident: it is not simply—as one might expect—God, the Infinite, the Unknown, the Eternal, who judges. On the

[2] *2 Clem.* 1, 1f.; cf. Kattenbusch 2:660.

contrary, he has handed the judgment over to one who, as man, is our brother. It is not a stranger who judges us but he whom we know in faith. The judge will advance to meet us, not as the entirely Other, but as one of us, who knows human existence from inside and has suffered.

Thus over the judgment glows the dawn of hope; it is not only the day of wrath but also the second coming of our Lord. One is reminded of the mighty vision of Christ with which the Book of Revelation begins (1:9–19): the seer sinks down as though dead before this being full of unearthly power. But the Lord lays his hand on him and says to him as once in the days when they were crossing the Lake of Gennesaret in wind and storm: "Fear not, it is I" (cf. 1:17). The Lord of all power is that Jesus whose comrade the visionary had once become in faith. The article in the Creed about the judgment transfers this very idea to our meeting with the Judge of the world. On that day of fear the Christian will be allowed to see in happy wonder that he to whom "all authority in heaven and on earth has been given" (Mt 28:18) was the companion in faith of his days on earth, and it is as if through the words of the Creed Jesus were already laying his hands on him and saying: Be without fear, it is I. Perhaps the problem of the intertwining of justice and mercy can be answered in no more beautiful way than it is in the idea that stands in the background of our Creed.

The Holy Spirit

Mind, Spirit, and Love

A Meditation on Pentecost

Is it really worth our while on feast days to pause for a moment and reflect on their meaning and, in the process, on the meaning of our own life, with its restlessness, hopes, and anxieties? Or is such a practice just a bourgeois custom, a desire for a bit of tinsel, a pious attempt to use earlier times as a means of "transfiguring" our own lives, and an attempt that we really ought to abandon once and for all?

For many people Pentecost is undoubtedly just a name for a long weekend on which they shift gears from everyday routine to leisure. They may spend the weekend endangering life and limb; in any case it is just as hectic and agitated for them as their typical weekday, but at least it offers the advantage of change, perhaps an illusion of freedom, perhaps even moments of real relaxation and satisfaction.

It would be foolish, of course, to look with condescending irony on weekends and the leisure they afford. Every one of us, after all, is happy about the chance for freedom that a weekend brings, even if views on how best to use the time surely differ greatly. And yet anyone who lives a

Translated by Matthew J. O'Connell and Michael J. Miller.

truly conscious life will be unable to settle for being passively driven from work to leisure and from leisure back to work again; now and then such a person must pause and ask where his life is leading and where mankind and the world as a whole are heading. He will have to accept his small share of responsibility for all this activity and its direction and not simply enjoy access to an ever wider selection of consumer goods without asking where it comes from and whither it is leading them.

Consequently, the person who is living with some degree of self-awareness will surely not regard reflection on a feast as so incredibly outmoded and purposeless as it might seem at first glance. When Pentecost comes around, he can remind himself, first of all, that in one form or another this feast has to do with what we call "spirit". Even if the approach to Christian faith has become difficult, various reflections will be prompted in this way.

What, then, is really meant by "spirit"? Today we encounter "spirit" chiefly as the rational mind that calculates and deals with the kind of stored-up knowledge that the computer can collect and manipulate; the mind that plans and in the process turns us into parts of a gigantic apparatus that no one can grasp in its entirety any longer but that moves forward and makes human beings both now and in their future an increasingly calculable element in an all-embracing whole.

When we hear this kind of talk and see the prospect opening before us of a mathematized world in which the last traces of romanticism have been swept away, then, despite all our hopes and expectations, we may well feel dismayed. For, even though we cannot deny the advantages, the comfort, the hopes, and everything great and liberating that the rationalization of the world has produced, yet we spontaneously understand statements like those of Jean Rostand: "I am so afraid of the natural sciences precisely because my

faith is in them alone",[1] or of Henri Bergson, who in con-
templating the vast technological development that the twentieth century has witnessed came to the conclusion that the
human race today "has too big a body for its soul".[2]

But the question then arises: Is the reality of "spirit" really
coextensive with what we have been describing, or does it
reach farther? Is spirit to be found only in the "positivistic"
form of the computer, or does it also take the form of what
Bergson calls "soul"? In fact, do we perhaps encounter the
real meaning and phenomenon of spirit, the element that is
decisive and liberating, only when we move beyond the kind
of "spirit" that can be stored in computers? Here we approach
once again the threshold of decision that Pentecost challenges us to cross. It takes a decision to move from weekend
to feast, from the simple use of the machinery of consum-
erism to reflection on it. It takes a further decision to pass
from the calculating spirit at work in the science of planning
to something greater that is admittedly more hidden as well.

Pierre-Henri Simon suggests that in dealing with all we
have been describing thus far, we should speak about "mind"
rather than about "spirit". Mind, then, is the sum of the
receptive, logical, and pragmatic powers of consciousness.
Spirit, on the other hand, discovers the order of values
that lies beyond facts, the freedom that transcends law, the
kind of existence in which justice has priority over self-
interest.[3] Spirit, thus understood, is not the object of calculation and computer storage; it is correlated precisely with
what is incalculable. It is a name for an attitude "that brings
fulfillment and happiness to the self by bursting through
the limitations of self-centeredness"; an attitude, in other

[1] Quoted from P.-H. Simon, *Woran ich glaube* (Tübingen, 1967), 176; to
this important book I owe the initial ideas for the present meditation.

[2] Cited in Simon, 180.

[3] Ibid., 175–83.

words, that requires a decision of the heart, of the whole human being.

When a person reaches this threshold, he has, of course, not yet reached the Christian message of Pentecost. The decision, as I have been describing it, for "spirit" over against positivism is one that even non-Christians can make; it is within the power of the whole human race. At the same time, however, the decision does represent the point at which people today will become capable of understanding once again what is meant by Christian faith in the Creator Spirit who renews the earth.

To most of our contemporaries and often even to those of them who mean to be believing Christians, the Pentecost message of the Bible and of those who preach it sounds like the stammering of a drunkard or the unintelligible babbling of dreamers who have not yet noticed that we have emerged into the daylight of the modern era, in which such talk is no longer acceptable. The people who react in this way hardly realize that in the confrontation between the "positive" and the "spiritual", between individuals who only serve the great machine and those who despite everything believe in contemplation and love, in truth and the abiding values that it yields—that in this confrontation they are, in the last analysis, face to face with the reality of Pentecost. When all is said and done, the urgent question of our time is whether the human race is to be saved by the perfecting of the "apparatus" or whether, on the contrary, Pascal's words still hold true: "All bodies together, and all minds together, and all their works, are of less worth than the smallest act of charity." [4]

[4] Pascal, *Pensées*, fragment 829 in *Oeuvres complètes*, ed. J. Chevalier (Paris: Bibliothèque de la Pléiade, 1954), 1341f. Cf. the thorough analysis of this passage in R. Guardini, *Christliches Bewusstsein: Versuche über Pascal*, 2nd ed. (Munich, 1950), 40ff. and 101ff.

But let us come at last to the main question. What is the real Christian message of Pentecost? What is this "Holy Spirit" of which it speaks? The Acts of the Apostles gives us an answer in the form of an image; perhaps there is no other way of expressing it, since the reality of the Spirit largely escapes our grasp. It relates that the disciples were touched by fiery tongues and found themselves speaking in a manner that some (the "positivists") regarded as drunken stammering, a meaningless, useless babbling, while each of the others, people from all parts of the then known world, heard the disciples speaking in his own tongue.

In the background of this text is the Old Testament story of the tower of Babel; taken together with this, the Acts of the Apostles provides us with a penetrating insight into the theology of history. The Old Testament account tells us that men, their sense of independence augmented by the progress they had made, attempted to build a tower that would reach heaven. That is, they believed that by their own powers of planning and constructing they could even build a bridge to heaven, make heaven accessible to themselves by their own efforts, and turn man into a deity. The result of their effort was the confusion of tongues. The human race, which seeks only itself and looks for salvation in the satisfaction of a ruthless egoism by means of economic power, suffers instead the consequence of egoism, which is the radical opposition of each to his fellows, so that no one understands the other any longer and consequently even egoism remains unfulfilled.

The New Testament account of Pentecost takes up these same ideas. It implies the conviction that contemporary mankind is sundered to its very roots; that it is characterized by a superficial coexistence and a hostility that are based on self-divinization. As a result, everything is seen in a false perspective; man ends up understanding neither God nor the world nor his fellowman nor himself. The "Holy Spirit" creates such an understanding because he is the Love that flows from the Cross, from the self-renunciation of Jesus Christ.

We need not attempt here to reflect in detail on the various dogmatic connections that are implied in such a description. For our purpose it is enough to recall the way Augustine tried to sum up the essential point of the Pentecost narrative. World history, he says, is a struggle between two kinds of love: self-love to the point of hatred for God, and love of God to the point of self-renunciation. This second love brings the redemption of the world and the self.[5]

In my opinion, it would already be a giant step forward if during the days of Pentecost we were to turn from the thoughtless use of our leisure to a reflection on our responsibility; if these days were to become the occasion for moving beyond purely rational thinking, beyond the kind of knowledge that is used in planning and can be stored up, to a discovery of "spirit", of the responsibility that truth brings, and of the values of conscience and love. Even if for the moment we did not find our way to Christianity, strictly speaking, we would already be touching the hem of Christ and his Spirit. In the long run, after all, "truth" and "love" cannot subsist in a vacuum, without relation to other things. If they are the timeless measure and the real hope of man, then they are not simply a part of the ever-changing historical scene but rather the point of reference for the movement of history. They are not remote ideas but have a face and a name. They issue a call to us. For they are "Love", that is to say, a person.

[5] Concerning Augustine's evaluation of the opposition between Babylon and Pentecost, see J. Ratzinger, *Die Einheit der Nationen* (Salzburg and Munich, 1971), 71–106.

The Holy Spirit is truly "spirit" in the fullest possible sense of the word. In all probability we must make our stumbling way to him anew from the midst of a profoundly changed world. Many, perhaps, will think it impossible to travel that way to the end, that is, to the "sober drunkenness" of Pentecostal faith. But the urgent question raised by Pentecost, a question that disturbs that terrible "sleep of conscience" of which Pierre-Henri Simon speaks,[6] is one that should and could apply to us all. The mighty wind of Pentecost blows on all of us, even today, especially today.

[6] Ibid., 190.

One, Holy, Catholic, and Apostolic Church

Church as the Locus of Service to the Faith

The word "Church" does not sound the way it used to; the good name is gone today. We are in almost the same position as the people in the last century of the Middle Ages, whose impression of the Church was summed up in the call for a reform of the Church in her head and members. Every day we hear about new shortcomings of her officials: one minute we are disturbed by the obstinacy of those who defend tradition, and the next minute we nevertheless have to shake our heads again over the high-handedness of others who on account of their personal problems think they have to raise the alarm in public. The institutions of the Church seem antiquated to us, often petty; a modern consciousness of human rights and insights into the social consequences of the Christian message are making headway only with effort. We often get the impression that some demands of the Church that are (or could quite easily become) outmoded are being defended with an undiscerning stubbornness that lays burdens on people instead

Translated by Michael J. Miller.

of helping them to be free; Jesus' judgments on the scribes
and Pharisees then come to mind, and we have the impression that they apply to those who serve the Church no
less than to those who served the synagogue. Conversely,
we also observe once more a peculiar opportunism of the
Church with regard to the trends of the times; she is suddenly inclined to accommodate where she ought to put
up resistance, and again and again we get the impression
that she is all too much in thrall to the mentality of certain groups that prevent her from being a force for unification and reconciliation, which of course should be her
task. Add to all that the fact that the scandals of Church
history are ceaselessly laid at our door. Slogans like Inqui-
sition, witch trials, persecution of the Jews, and so on, are
household words today for every last one of our contemporaries, noticeably creating the general impression that the
Church of the past was in any case a failure and that if the
Church is worth any commitment at all, one must make a
clean break with everything that has come before and start
over from the beginning.

But can we actually put any trust in such new promises?
Who is vouching, then, for the quality of the Church of
the future? And based on what? One might argue: If no
lasting good could come from the work of Jesus and the
apostles, then who are the prophets to whom we can entrust
ourselves now? Thus, a commitment to a Church that is
now finally becoming quite different inevitably seems like
an unsecured bill of exchange, with no convincing arguments to encourage us to sign it. And for all these reasons
the courage to devote one's whole life to the service of the
Church is fading away more and more.

What are we supposed to say about it? Perhaps it is good
to look first at what our faith itself has formulated from
within as an answer to such questions. This answer says that

the Church is "strength in weakness", a combination of human failure and divine mercy. Next, it is part of the Church's nature that she is divine and human, rich and poor, light and dark all at once. God became a beggar and entered so much into solidarity with the prodigal son that he appears downright identical to him, that he himself is the other, precisely that lost and prodigal son upon whom all the vices of history are laid. According to the proclamation of the faith, the Church, precisely as a sinful society, is the expression of the Divine Mercy, of God's solidarity with sinners. That in turn means that she is, on the one hand, debased by all human failure, yet at the same time something from God is preserved within her and remains effective, giving man hope and salvation. According to this account, then, the Church is by nature "paradoxical", dimorphic, a mixture of failings and blessings.

The urgent question arises: Is that so? I believe one certainly can recognize the truth of these statements by examining the situation with a modicum of patience and objectivity. For besides the Church history of scandals that is drummed into us so relentlessly nowadays, there is also the other Church history, which is a story of hope, a path of light starting from Jesus and becoming now wider, now narrower, but never completely disappearing as it goes through the centuries. Let us remember just a few details so as to snatch this other Church history back from oblivion. We can hardly imagine today what it meant in 217 for a slave in Rome to become pope. According to the law of the ancient world, a slave was regarded, not as a person, but as a thing. In the Church, however, he was a brother and, as brother, equal. This peculiar feature of the Church was so strong, in comparison with the old pagan society, that it could have far-reaching consequences in events that were, indeed, only a symptom of the power of the Christian revolution, which achieved its effects, not by terror, but by an interior transformation. A few centuries later, when the ancient world collapsed under the Germanic onslaughts, the Christian faith again proved to be the decisive force for reconciliation, which managed to bring together the new world of the conquerors and the old world of a great but weary culture, so that the conquerors and the vanquished, the barbarians and the heirs of the wealth of ancient culture saw one another in turn as brothers and became capable of building a new world together. Through the message of the faith, both sides came to see that they belonged to one single God and not to different hostile deities, that they were loved equally by their one brother Jesus Christ, and that he had suffered for the one people as well as for the other. Augustine, who saw the Vandal attack upon Africa coming and died during the siege of his diocesan city, had pointed out more than once that the peace of Christ extends farther than the power of the Roman Empire to keep the peace and that the faith could and must embrace barbarians and Romans equally.

Then in the High Middle Ages, from within a Church that had become wealthy and identified with society, the pristine figure of Saint Francis emerged, who was a magnificent example of a Christian critique of society: voluntary solidarity with the poor, which distinguished the faith from the ruling powers, is one side of his program, while the idea of peace is the other—both inner peace as opposed to the disorder of the power struggles among the various strata of medieval society and also external peace: mission as opposed to crusade, striving for unity in the world based on God's unity. Naturally, these initiatives had only very fragmentary consequences politically, but they were there; they were lively forces that appeared on the scene again and again by virtue of the Church's living faith.

These statements are true even for the darkest hours of Church history: Amid the horrible incidents of the Spanish colonization of America, men like the Dominican priest Las Casas rose up, who relentlessly fought for the human rights of the oppressed. It must be said, to the credit of the Spanish crown, that they listened seriously to such voices and tried again and again, with various approaches, to create a colonial law based on respect for human beings, even though they lacked the power to ensure that that law, which was Christian in its inspiration, would be accepted in the other hemisphere. Out of this struggle, and long before the Enlightenment, Spanish Scholasticism developed the concept of international law by which we still live today. The faith of the Church was, admittedly, misused again and again as a pretext for the pursuit of personal and national claims to power, but at the same time this faith always remained, nevertheless, the prophetic salt that rankled and disturbed the mighty. The cry for liberty, equality, and fraternity that became increasingly intense in the modern era is incomprehensible without the faith that was preserved in the Church.

The Church's faith was expressed, however, in still another way that is more difficult for us to see and yet no less decisive. Man does not live on bread alone—we really ought to know that very well today, in a time when people have enjoyed their prosperity *ad nauseam*, so that they now revolt not against poverty but against prosperity. Someone who is as well-fed as can be and can afford everything he wants starts to notice that that is still much too little. If someday everybody has everything they want, they will still be far from happy. On the contrary, the Western world of today proves that then they are just beginning to be completely unhappy, that that is when their problems really start. To that extent, man cannot be redeemed by bread and money.

He hungers for more. The escape into drugs, which is now becoming a mass phenomenon, demonstrates this all too clearly. The Church through all those centuries gave people an awareness of their intrinsic dignity that no one could take from them: along with the gift of hope, she gave them the meaning of faith, which makes them rich and free. It is quite obvious how foolish it is to describe all that as "the opiate of the people", now that the people do in fact take opium precisely because they have the prosperity that is supposed to make the opiate superfluous.

And furthermore: figures like Vincent de Paul or Mary Ward, or whatever the names of the many modern founders of religious orders may be, show that the Christian faith not only negatively provoked protests that are critical of society but also positively gave individuals the strength to serve, without which a society is doomed to decline. Today, when we Germans have to recruit nuns from Yugoslavia, Spain, or even from India and Korea to staff our hospitals and nursing homes (although Asia itself could urgently use its personnel), this points up a shortage in our society that very soon will probably have weightier consequences than the much debated "education shortage", which tends to mistake spiritless schooling for education and forgets about the achievement of a human being. With money you can buy a lot, but not the spirit of selfless service; you can perhaps borrow that for a time from other nations, but if it is permanently lacking in the social organism of a people, its accomplishments stand on clay feet, and its collapse is unavoidable in the long term. Here we can see that a people cannot live on its production alone (as the naive materialism of our public opinion supposes) but rather needs intellectual and spiritual forces in order to continue. People today smile or even laugh at the fact that the Church throughout the centuries has inspired the strength to serve and has been able to impart meaning to that service. Thus "undemocratic" virtues such as humility, patience, the voluntary restriction of one's own freedom for the sake of another's freedom, in the view of our progressive contemporaries, at best prove how reactionary those who practice them are or even prompt the critics to label them "the fashioning of idols", as though these virtues benefited only the ruling powers. "They are beneficial to the suffering", one ought to reply—but probably the laughter and the smiles in this regard will soon pass anyway.

Let us return to our starting point. Perhaps the observations that we have tried to make about the "other Church history" may sound rather apologetic. Nevertheless, it is simply necessary now and then to recall facts that are ignored or repressed; the suspicion about "apologetics" is not infrequently just one part of the repression that resists remembering. There is the approach in which anything dark is repressed—that is supposedly "apologetics"; there is also, however, the opposite approach in which one is willing to see only what is dark so as to be entirely liberated from the past, but in that way, too, man falls into self-deception and loses his way. If we are trying to be realistic, we must acknowledge both: in the Church there is the constant darkness of serious human failure, but in her also abides a hope that man needs in order to be able to live. One might say she is like fertile farmland on which the best wheat grows if it is tended; if it is neglected, however, it can also become a collection of all sorts of weeds. Or to use another image: she is like a people with great talents; such a people can become a blessing if it uses its gifts correctly; it can also become a curse if it misunderstands them.

This is the basis of our responsibility for the Church. She is God's planting, as faith tells us, but to a very large extent she is also left in our hands, so that the weeds can overrun the wheat, the olive tree can put forth leaves and remain fruitless—to use images from the Bible. However, the question of what is to become of the Church is not as indifferent as the fate of some pigeon breeders' association, the formation or disappearance of which we note without any particular emotion. For preserved in the Church are the sources of spiritual power for human life, without which this life becomes empty and society disintegrates. In the explosive situation in which we find ourselves today, mankind no doubt needs an abundant supply of technological know-how in order to make coexistence and survival possible. But by technological know-how alone it cannot be saved, for it makes new possibilities for production and new possibilities for destruction available simultaneously; indeed, the possibilities for production are often just as easily possibilities for destruction. If along with the increase in technological know-how the spiritual reservoirs of mankind dry up, then it is doomed to self-destruction. Mankind needs a framework of meaning that imparts the strength to serve, that creates an interior freedom from the world and thereby gives individuals the ability to live and work unselfishly, because a man's hope is more deeply rooted than his external career aspirations. Yet all that cannot last without the mighty force of a living faith that is in itself disinterested. In this regard, service to the faith is an existential need for man, even today and especially today. The technician who strives to find new possibilities of material survival and the believer who is at the service of the faith and seeks new ways of spiritual survival are working at two sides of one and the same common task. They should not allow themselves to be played off against each other, but rather extend to one another a helping hand with the one project they serve.

From all that has been said, it should probably be obvious that no service is rendered to anyone by a Church that we make for ourselves, one that is cut off from her spiritual foundations. Conversely, it should be no less clear that the Church needs our commitment in the struggle to bring forth good fruit on her land and that this is a task for mankind as a whole.

The Communion of Saints

What Do the Saints Really Mean for Us?

How is it that in the liturgy they enter into our meeting with the living God? We can get an answer from Saint Augustine: Through the saints God reminds us of himself. Of course mankind's memory of God is not entirely lost. But one of the consequences of what we call man's state of original sin is that this memory has become very dim, very pale, very erratic, ineffective, and vague.

In the flood of images and information that presses in on us every day, he is practically indiscernible. He has no meaning; he does not seem to be present or important in the real life of people. Admittedly, there is an uneasiness in man; he is aware that he lacks something, that he is called to something great, and this uneasiness keeps him on the move, as though he were looking for a forgotten word without which he will not be at peace. Especially in our era, with the vehemence of its explosions and all its attempts to arrive at the fulfillment of humanity, we sense that something is at work in man, that he is seeking that great, unknown thing to which he knows he is called.

Translated by Michael J. Miller.

Saint Augustine once said in this connection that there are two sorts of forgetting. One consists of this: even if someone tells me about the forgotten thing and tries to bring it back, it is useless. The matter has completely escaped me; it has left no trace; it is no longer there. In the other sort of forgetting, I again do not know about the thing that has sunk into oblivion, but when someone comes and reminds me, it can, as it were, be brought forth from the deep caverns of the unconscious. So it is with forgetting God. Man cannot entirely lose him from his life, because God himself is there at the bottom of his soul. But of course in our consciousness he can be covered over, so that we need reminding. God has responded to this situation of ours, in which a reminder must help out our fading memory. In his Son he himself has entered into the perceptible world; he puts himself visibly and audibly in our way, so to speak; he refreshes our memory, so that the lost word arises again from the bottom of our soul, so that in Christ he himself might be always present and close to us.

So that this call might be present at all times, Christ comes to meet us through the saints, people who have lived on this remembrance and thereby have themselves become reminders of God. Losing the remembrance of God means forgetting life, Augustine once said. Only when this remembrance returns do we begin again to live at all, does the essential part of our self become present to us again. Hence the resurfacing of the remembrance of God is more than a forgotten telephone number, a name, or a word coming to mind again. It means that my being is set right again, sees the light again, comes back to itself, back to life. This coming of the remembrance of God within me we call conversion. Every Christian must be a convert or, more precisely, must walk along the way of conversion. Now we all say this, but silently we think to ourselves: conversion, good, that is something for the so-called converts, for people who have lived apart from God for a time and who rediscover him and reorient their lives toward him. But what is conversion supposed to mean for someone who from the beginning was introduced to the faith and has always tried, more or less successfully and piously, to live it? If we think like that, we have not understood the word conversion correctly. A good twenty years after his conversion Saint Augustine wrote in his book on the Trinity, based on the experience of those twenty years, the sentence: "Ista renovatio non uno conversionis momento fit" (This renewal does not take place in one moment of conversion). The remembrance we are talking about cannot come about in a single moment of conversion but, rather, is the path of an entire life. For life is not over and done in a moment, and hence the rectification of a life can be accomplished only in the totality of this path. Let us look once again at ourselves. Certainly we know about God; we know more or less the truths of our faith; we are familiar with all this intellectually. But do we not have to admit that, given the way we lead our lives, God's presence every so often slips from our memory, that we go on living as though we had forgotten him, that he is simply not there in our living memory? And do we not all, therefore, need again and again for him to stand in the way of our senses, as it were, to touch our face, to speak in our hearing, and thereby to make remembrance come alive and thus give us life?—a life that continues to march onward and that, therefore, is not over until death but, rather, continues to be conversion until death. A further point is connected with this. The remembrance of God that is our lot means that the light of truth falls into my life; that the path through the fog-bound world in which we find ourselves is enlarged; that I do not just receive some information, but rather see how things are; that the real truth, the truth about the world and about my life, dawns within me. Today the word "truth" has almost disappeared from our religious vocabulary. We all talk about values, even about religious values, and almost everybody is in favor of having them around, too. But truth—that is too much for us, a demand that appears too lofty and too dangerous for us.

The modern age has inoculated us all with the conviction that we can have objective and therefore reliable and communicable knowledge about physics and technology but cannot really know and be certain about divine things. These are manifested to us—so the modern age supposes—only in a haze of different symbols that do not allow us to say: This is true and that is false. Instead, each individual has to figure out on his own how to deal with the situation. Religion is relegated to the realm of sentiment, feeling, and subjectivity. Everyone has only to look for what best serves to satisfy his religious feelings, so that he can keep this department of his existence in equilibrium as well. But a religion that is understood in this way is much like a lump of clay that can be shaped and turned at will. If it demands something of us, we turn away indignantly. For we called on it in the first place to make things more comfortable, so as to get something out of it, not so as to let troublesome demands into our life. Or to use a different image: in the supermarket of ideas and ideologies, everyone looks for the items on his list and loads up his own basket with what speaks to him, with what he thinks will help him cope and make his life somewhat more pleasant. But in a religion of this sort, in which we ourselves gather only what suits us, the self remains the final standard. We have not even begun to take conversion seriously; instead, we really worship only ourselves, and God becomes the means for fulfilling our own wishes, that is, we do not let him be God.

Becoming a Christian, Christian conversion, however, consists precisely of getting out of this type of rubber religion and recognizing that the light of truth itself is falling into my life. Truth manifests itself as it is; God manifests himself in his Son and becomes for me the Way. And because in God truth and will are one, this means that this truth is binding, that I step into the void, in other words, into what is untrue and dishonest if I walk past it or push it aside, that I am alive only if I give my will over to the will of God. Only in this way does conversion become true; only in this way does the remembrance of God arrive in me and create life for me. Precisely through troubles, this remembrance purifies me and leads me to the truth about myself and to fulfillment in the true love for which our existence is constantly on the lookout.

One last thing must be added to what we have said: Augustine had already received the remembrance of God quite some time before he was able to make up his mind to convert, before he became capable of pronouncing the *Yes* of the whole man who not only knows something about God in his intellect but gives his will over to the will of God and thereby becomes true. The will does not simply do what the intellect knows, but why is that so?

In the later years of his life, Augustine kept pondering this remarkable state of affairs and left us important insights into it. He grasped that the will is free and not free at the same time, that in fact it cannot simply do what knowledge might recommend to it; rather, the will is, as he says, embedded in our emotions and sentiments, in what we would call the unconscious and preconscious preliminary decisions of our life, our passions, our feelings.

If God wants the remembrance of him really to break through and to become the way in us, then it is not enough for him to manifest himself to our intellect. Rather, he has to enter into the depths of our feelings, of our emotional, preconscious decisions and make himself present there, for they can be the lead weight that drags us down, but they can also become the wings through which we can reach the heights and the open air. And this is the most profound center of the mystery of God, of the God who takes upon himself the trouble of reminding.

He has touched not only our understanding but our hearts.

He has shown that he is kind. Only when we begin to love God, that is, only when we begin to recognize that the truth is worth living, that the Commandments are not an external imposition but, rather, are in the service of love, only when we learn to see this in Christ does our will become free; only then do we become converts; then life really begins in us.

Let us ask the Lord to allow this to happen to us, to show himself to us in a way that reaches into our heart and our feelings and thus makes our intellect and will free.

Let us ask him to grant us real conversion, day by day, so that we might learn to live. Amen.

The Forgiveness of Sins

Metanoia as the Fundamental Datum of Christian Existence

Introduction: The problem

When one tries to translate the word *metanoia*, one immediately runs into difficulties: change of mind, reconsider-
ing, remorse, repentance, turning back, conversion are
available, but none of these words exhausts the contents of
the original meaning, even though turning back and conversion indicate most clearly the radical character of what
we are talking about: a process that affects one's whole life
and affects life wholly, that is, definitively, in the totality
of its temporal extent, and that means far more than just
one single or even a repeated act of thinking, feeling, or
willing. Perhaps the difficulty of finding a linguistic equivalent is connected also with the fact that the designated
matter has become foreign to us, appears to us only in
scattered pieces but no longer as a comprehensive whole.
And there is a peculiar strangeness even about the individual pieces that remain. Now admittedly today hardly
anyone would still repeat Nietzsche's statement: "'Sin'...

Translated by Michael J. Miller.

is a Jewish feeling and a Jewish invention. Regarding this background, ... Christianity did aim to 'Judaize' the whole world. How far it has succeeded in Europe is brought out by the fact that Greek antiquity—a world without feelings of sin—still seems so very strange to our sensibility.... 'Only if you *repent* will God show you grace'—that would strike a Greek as ridiculous and annoying." [1]

Yet even though this scoffing at the idea of sin and repentance as something Jewish is understandably no longer current, the basic sentiment is still prevalent and no less forceful today. A second passage from Nietzsche that I would like to cite in this connection could almost as easily be found in the work of any modern theologian: "In the whole psychology of the 'Gospels', the concepts of guilt and punishment are lacking.... 'Sin', which means anything that puts distance between God and man, is abolished—this is precisely the 'glad tidings'." [2]

The attempt to give Christianity new publicity value by setting it without qualification in a positive relation to the world, indeed, by portraying it as conversion to the world, suits our feelings about life and hence is becoming increasingly widespread. Many false fears about sinning, which were created by a narrow-minded moral theology and perhaps not that infrequently fostered and spread by spiritual direction, are taking their revenge today and make the Christianity of the past appear to many people as a torment that constantly brought man into conflict with himself instead of setting him free for open and fearless cooperation with all people of good will. One might almost say that the words sin, remorse, and repentance are among the new

[1] *The Gay Science*, trans. Walter Kaufmann (New York: Random House, 1974), par. 135, p. 187.

[2] *The Antichrist*, trans. H. L. Mencken (New York: Knopf, 1920), 101f.

taboos with which modern consciousness defends itself from the power of the dark questions that could become dangerous to its self-assured pragmatism.

Admittedly, the general scene in this regard also has changed again already within the past three or four years. The all-too-naive progressivism in the years immediately after the Council, which cheerfully pledged solidarity with everything that is modern and promising and strove with the eagerness of the star pupil to prove that Christianity is compatible with everything modern and to demonstrate the loyalty of Christians to the trends in today's life—that progressivism today has already come under the suspicion of being just an apotheosis of late-capitalistic conventionality, to which it adds a religious gleam instead of destroying it critically. Now here a relatively modest little demon is being replaced by seven worse ones that board from the rear, yet the disillusionment can be salutary. For in the garish lightning of the storm that is stirred up by such criticism, it is nonetheless unmistakably clear that man's existence and his world are not really making progress so pleasantly and smoothly that one could simply convert to this same world—in order to serve it, one must criticize it, one must change it. A Christianity that regards proving its piety in all respects according to the standards of the day as its only remaining task has nothing to say and no importance. It can just step aside. Those who live in today's world with their eyes open, who recognize its contradictions and its destructive tendencies—from the self-defeating consequences of technology in polluting the environment to the self-defeating behavior of society in its problems with race and class—do not expect a Christian affirmation but rather the prophetic salt that stings, burns, accuses, and transforms. With that, nevertheless, a fundamental aspect of metanoia has moved into our field of vision—for it requires a change in man in order for salvation to come about. The ideology of accommodation is not what saves Christianity, an ideology that is still at work in places where with trendy eagerness or belated courage people criticize those institutions that are powerless anyway and have become the refuse of the world (whereby they incidentally follow the apostolic model once more: 1 Cor 4:13);[3] the only thing that can help Christianity is the prophetic courage to bring its own voice decisively and unmistakably to bear on the present hour.

Although the social and public component of metanoia begins to come into view again here, there are plenty of signs that point up the indispensability of conversion, of turning back and its visible signs, in the individual human being. In Protestant Christian circles, Frank Buchmann rediscovered, for the movement of moral rearmament that he founded, the necessity of confession as an act of liberation, the need for becoming new, for leaving the past and the destructive enclosure of guilt behind and entering into one's own; in the secular field, psychotherapy in its own way has stumbled onto the fact that unconquered guilt divides a human being, destroys him spiritually and at last bodily as well, and that there is no way to overcome this without the confrontation that sets loose what is repressed and rankling within and brings it to a confession. The increasing numbers of such secular father-confessors should make it plain even to a blind man that sin is no Jewish invention but rather the burden of all human beings. It is the real burden from which in most cases they have to be liberated if they want and are to become free.

[3] See Hans Urs von Balthasar, *Elucidations*, trans. John Riches (San Francisco: Ignatius Press, 1998), 310–14.

On the basic biblical meaning of metanoia

In view of these profane fragments of the fundamental experience of metanoia that appear now before our eyes on every side, the question of what Christian metanoia really means now becomes quite urgent. The symposium for which this paper was written is elaborating the particular aspects of this question; here we can only attempt an initial outline of its spiritual profile. As we have heard, Nietzsche made sin and remorse out to be something typically Jewish, and in contrast he ascribed to the Greeks a noble courage that found beauty in wantonness, too, and considered remorse ridiculous. Greek tragedy, which he mentions as evidence for this, proves the opposite upon closer inspection: a horror of the power of a curse, which even the gods are incapable of averting.[4] Anyone who even glances at the history of religion will recognize the extent to which it is dominated by the theme of guilt and atonement and what abstruse and often weird attempts men have made to cleanse themselves from the burdensome feeling of guilt without really being able to get free. In order to bring the special characteristics of biblical metanoia into the picture, we will venture to make only two small observations here. In classical and Hellenistic Greek, the word *metanoia* acquired no clear physiognomy. The verb μετανοεῖν means "to perceive afterward, to change one's mind, to regret, to feel remorse, to be sorry"; the substantive form, accordingly, means "change of mind, remorse, regret". "A change of one's entire moral attitude, a thoroughgoing change in one's way of life, a conversion

---

[4] Cf., for example, the penetrating analyses in G. Murray, *Euripides and His Age* (London and New York: Oxford Univ. Press, 1965); Hans Urs von Balthasar, *The Glory of the Lord: A Theological Aesthetics*, vol. 4: *The Realm of Metaphysics in Antiquity*, trans. Brian McNeil, C.R.V., et al. (San Francisco: Ignatius Press, 1989), 101–154.

that henceforth defines one's whole behavior are not what
Hellenism has in mind by μετάνοια. A Greek can μετανοεῖν
a sin *in actu* in his own sight or in the presence of the gods
... , [but] he is unacquainted with μετάνοια as repentance
or conversion as those terms are used in the Old and New
Testaments."[5] Individual acts of metanoia remain individual acts of regret or remorse; they do not add up to a whole,
to an abiding, comprehensive turn of one's entire life onto
a new path: metanoia is just remorse and does not become
conversion. The fact that all of existence *as a whole* is in
need of that one single conversion in order to be itself does
not become evident. Perhaps one might say that the difference between polytheism and monotheism is silently at work
here as well: an existence that relies on many divine powers
and attempts to assert itself in the confusion and conflict
among them can only be a multifarious game with the ruling forces, whereas the one God becomes the one way that
sets man before the Yes or No of turning toward or turning away and gathers his existence into a single call.

Here an objection arises that can again, at the same time,
clarify what we mean. For one could say that the arguments thus far apply only as long as we limit ourselves exclusively to the connotations of μετάνοια—μετανοεῖν, whereas
they cease to be valid if we include the Greek word for
conversion, namely, ἐπιστροφή-ἐπιστρέφιν (the Septuagint quite
appropriately used this word, in most cases, for the Hebrew
šūb).[6] With the word στρέφειν, Plato designates the circular

[5] J. Behm, "μετανοέω, μετάνοια", in *ThWNT* 972–1004, citation at 975f.;
on the meaning of the word, see especially 972–75.

[6] Ibid., 985ff. The significance of this, however, is missed in Behm's presentation, which is entirely under the spell of schematic oppositions: biblical
vs. Greek, the law vs. the prophets, cult vs. personal religiosity, and thus,
despite a comprehensive review of the material, is dubious in its evaluations
as well as in its classification of the phenomenon. The schematic form of

movement, that is, the perfect movement belonging to the gods, the heavens, and the world. The circle, which is initially a cosmic symbol, thus becomes at the same time an existential symbol: the sign for the return of existence to itself. Based on this original sense, ἐπιστροφή becomes for the Stoics and in Neoplatonism a return to the unity of reality, a soaring ascent into the great circular form of the world, the central moral postulate.[7] Thereby one arrives at the insight that the human being, in order truly to find the way to himself, needs the comprehensive movement of turning back and turning within, which as a permanent task of conversion challenges him to gather up his life from distraction by external things and to recollect himself in interiority, where truth dwells. In my opinion, a false concern about the originality of the Bible or a naive opposition of biblical to Greek thought certainly need not lead us to deny that philosophical thinking here is on the way to Christian faith and provides a formula in which the Church Fathers were able to express the ontological depth of the historical process of Christian conversion. Let us say confidently, then: There is a convergence here. But we must add that with this reference to man's turning in toward himself the ancient Greeks have not yet arrived at the full extent of the conversion that is demanded by the Bible. For the Greek term ἐπιστροφή turns inward, toward that innermost depth of the human being which is one thing and everything at the same time. It is idealistic: if a man goes deep enough, he hits upon what is divine within himself. The faith of the Bible is more critical, more radical.

Behm's article is simply adopted by P. Hoffmann, "Umkehr", in *Handbuch theologischer Grundbegriffe*, ed. H. Fries, 2:719–24 (Munich, 1963).

[7] Cf. the painstaking commentary by P. Hadot, "Conversio", in *Historisches Wörterbuch der Philosophie*, ed. J. Ritter, 1:1033–36 (Stuttgart, 1981).

It criticizes not just the external man. It knows that danger can result precisely from the arrogance of the mind, of man's interiority, and of his depth. It criticizes not only half of man but the whole. Salvation does not come from interiority alone, for this very interiority can be rigid, domineering, egotistical, or wicked. "What comes out of a man is what defiles a man" (Mk 7:20). What saves is not simply turning toward self but rather turning away from self to the God who calls. Thus man does not rely on the ultimate depth of his self but, rather, on the God who approaches from outside, on the "thou" that breaks him open and in that very process redeems him. That is why metanoia means the same thing as obedience and faith; that is why it is part of the framework of the covenant reality; that is why it is related to the communion of those who are called to follow the same way. Where there is faith in the personal God, horizontality and verticality, interiority and service are not irreducibly opposed. And so it is clear at the same time that metanoia is not just some sort of Christian attitude but, rather, is actually the fundamental Christian act, understood, of course, in terms of one very definite aspect: the aspect of change, the act of turning, of becoming new and different. In order to become a Christian, a human being must change, not merely in one place or another, but unconditionally, down to the very bottom of his being.

Change and fidelity

With that we have arrived at a point that is very important precisely for the modern mind-set as well. For the concepts "change" and "progress" are surrounded today by a positively religious aura. Salvation comes only through change; calling somebody a conservative is the equivalent of an

excommunication from society, because in current parlance
it is tantamount to saying that he is opposed to progress,
closed off from the new, and thus a defender of what is old,
obscure, and servile, an enemy of the salvation that is
expected from change. Does metanoia point in the same
direction? Finally, was Christianity, which is based on the
fundamental act of metanoia, a similarly all-encompassing
struggle for change when it first appeared in history, only
later congealing like lava, which turns from fire into hard
stone? How is the Christian willingness to change, that is,
metanoia, related to the modern will to change? Dietrich
von Hildebrand, who is known nowadays almost exclusively for his *Trojan Horse*,[8] wrote in an early work before
the [Second World] War a treatise on the Christian readiness to change[9] that is still remarkable today; on the one
hand, it reads like a calm justification for his conversion to
the Catholic faith, as an apologia for that great change in
his life which many people are unwilling to understand,
which appeared to be infidelity, a falling away from the faith
of his fathers. In this situation he presents a passionate plea
for a willingness to make a radical change, and in it, of
course, one can also hear quite clearly his No to the cult of
movement [*Kult der Bewegung*] that had come to power,
forcing him to have his book published under a pseud-
onym and then to leave the European continent. I think
that the inner unity of radical change and radical fidelity
that metanoia implies has rarely been formulated so lucidly
as in this essay, which was written simultaneously as an
apologia for the radical change he carried out and in opposition to the "mobility" that promised salvation for the world

[8] *Trojan Horse in the City of God* (Chicago: Franciscan Herald Press, 1967).
[9] Dietrich von Hildebrand, *Transformation in Christ* (New York: Longmans, Green & Co., 1948), 1–23.

through a revolutionary political movement and yet ended in terror and destruction that were historically unprecedented.

Therefore, in reference to our question, I would like simply and briefly to repeat Hildebrand's essential points and to relate them to their biblical basis somewhat more clearly than he does in his essay. As he explains it, the distinguishing feature of the Christian willingness to change is first of all its boundlessness, its radical character, which goes down to the very foundations. This distinguishes it from the attitude of the moral idealist: He wants to change in certain respects but does not allow himself to be called into question as far as his nature as a whole is concerned. And of course even the Christian all too easily gets stuck in such limited willingness to change, in all sorts of reservations, whereby he often exempts from change precisely that which needs it the most.

> Their conscience permits them to remain entrenched in their self-assertion. For example, they do not feel the obligation of loving their enemy; they let their pride have its way within certain limits; they insist on the right of giving play to their natural reactions in answer to any humiliation. They maintain as self-evident their claim to the world's respect, they dread being looked upon as "fools of Christ"—they accord a certain role to human respect and are anxious to stand justified in the eyes of the world also. They are not ready for a total breach with the world and its standards; they are swayed by certain conventional considerations; nor do they refrain from "letting themselves go" within reasonable limits.[10]

Their metanoia remains ethical and particular; it does not become really Christian. When we consider, however, that becoming a Christian depends on the occurrence of really *Christian* metanoia, in the sense of prophetic preaching and of Jesus' preaching, then it is clear that this half-measure

[10] Ibid., 5.

metanoia is the real reason for today's crisis of Christianity: "They... are anxious to stand justified in the eyes of the world also. They are not ready for a total breach with the world"—this keeping one eye on what everybody thinks is ruining the Church today as it always has, but perhaps more today, because "everybody" now has different ways of exerting pressure. Unfortunately there is no disputing that even men of the Church today make their decisions, not simply according to what faith in Jesus Christ demands, but rather quite emphatically according to what "everybody" will say, so as to save face; once someone has gained the reputation of being a man of progress, he all too quickly becomes the prisoner of that reputation, which only apparently serves the cause of freedom but in truth leads to the slavery of vanity and destroys metanoia. The facetiously ironic saying by Wilhelm Busch ought to give Christians a little more courage to resist the pressure of prevailing standards: "Ist der Ruf erst ruiniert, lebt sich's fortan ungeniert" (Once your reputation is gone, life goes nonchalantly on"). The courage to make the break gives you freedom—it alone gives freedom. This courage to make the break is called, in biblical language, metanoia—but this is precisely the courage we lack. "*Complete* readiness for change is an indispensable precondition of the 'conception' of Christ in our souls." [11] This remark ought to frighten us: this is precisely the prophetic demand of Christ's forerunner, and the only path to Christ is by way of him.

The fluidity of existence that is consequently necessary is thus at the same time "far, then, from ... a glorification of movement as such...." [12] The willingness to change for the sake of following Christ has nothing to do with the lack of direction evident in the reed that is swayed by every wind; it

[11] Ibid., 23.
[12] Ibid., 9.

has nothing to do with an existential indecisiveness, a facile susceptibility to influence that allows itself to be pushed around in any direction. It is at the same time a process of becoming firm in Christ, "a hardening in relation to all tendencies toward being changed from below—a flexibility in relation to all formative influences 'from above'".[13] In other words: Christian metanoia is objectively identical to *pistis* (faith, fidelity), a change that does not exclude fidelity but, rather, makes it possible. The New Testament speaks about the irreversibility of the fundamental Christian decision with a severity that seems positively uncanny to us: "For it is impossible to restore again to repentance those who have once been enlightened, who have tasted the heavenly gift, and have become partakers of the Holy Spirit, and have tasted the goodness of the word of God and the powers of the age to come, if they then commit apostasy, since they crucify the Son of God on their own account and hold him up to contempt" (Heb 6:4–6). Someone who turns back from turning back goes backward instead of forward. Once the true direction, that is, the direction of truth has been found, it remains a direction, a way; it continues to be a destination and demands movement. But as a direction it is no longer replaceable, because from now on turning aside or turning back can only be turning away from the truth. Hildebrand correctly points out that this fidelity to the direction of truth that one has discovered is and must always be something fundamentally different from "formal conservatism": its persistence is based on the abiding validity of the truth. "The selfsame motive that impels the person with continuity to cling imperturbably to truth will equally commit him to be ready to accept every new truth." [14] This implies two things: it means, first,

[13] Ibid., 8.
[14] Ibid., 14.

that the Christian cannot leave behind metanoia or his willingness to change after he has become a Christian as though it were something from the past that no longer concerns him. There is still within him, after all, the tension between two gravitational forces: the gravitation of self-interest and egotism and the gravitation of truth, of love. The first is still his "natural" gravitation, which designates, so to speak, the more likely state of affairs. And the second force can remain within him only if he counteracts again and again the gravitation of selfish interests to follow the gravitation of truth and is willing to change accordingly and if he is ready, finally, to allow himself to be molded away from himself and into Christ. In this respect the fluidity of existence must not decrease but, rather, increase. At the same time this means that truth always remains a direction, a destination, and never becomes a possession that has been acquired definitively. Christ, who is the truth, is the way in this world precisely because he is the truth.

An observation from the history of language is pertinent here. As far as I can tell, the Latin word *proficere-profectus*, the verb "to pro*gress*" and the noun "*prog*ress", acquired a decidedly positive meaning and in general a clear semantic profile only in Christianity, but very early on.[15] The orations of the Roman Missal take it for granted that one should pray for Christians to *proficere*, to make progress; Vincent of Lerins has a treatise on progress in the knowledge of divine

[15] For the gradual development of the connotations of *progressus*, see M. Seckler, "Der Fortschrittsgedanke in der Theologie", in *Theologie im Wandel*, published by the Catholic Theological Faculty at the University of Tübingen, ed. J. Ratzinger and J. Neumann, 41–67, esp. 42f. (Munich, 1968); an extensive and nuanced presentation of the question (although without a detailed etymological investigation) can be found now in K. Thraede, "Fortschritt", in *Reallexikon für Antike und Christentum*, 8:141–82; cf. also E. von Ivanka, "Die Wurzeln des Fortschrittsglaubens in Antike und Mittelalter", in *Der Fortschrittsglaube: Sinn und Gefahren*, ed. U. Schöndorfer, 13–23 (Graz, 1966).

truth; Bonaventure finally coins the beautiful expression: "Christi opera non deficiunt, sed proficient" (Christ's works do not go backward but rather forward)—and with it he defends the new spiritual awakening of the mendicant orders against the conservatism of the secular clergy. The seed sown in apostolic work continues to grow through the ages until it attains the fullness of Christ.[16] Whereas antiquity is characterized by the circular pattern of *status-progressio-regressus*,[17] now that a direction has been found there can be "progress", and, indeed, only on that condition does it exist at all. "Progress" and "fidelity" are mutually dependent. Perhaps I can venture a comparison from the field of human relations in order to make this somewhat more concrete: Who is authentically growing as a man, who is advancing, going forward: the playboy who lurches from one fleeting encounter to the next and has no time at all really to encounter a "thou"? Or the man who carries through his Yes to another human being, goes forward with it, and in this Yes actually does not become rigid but rather learns slowly and ever more deeply therein to make himself available to the "thou" and thus actually to find freedom, truth, and love? Just to continue that Yes, once it is spoken, demands a constant willingness to change, one that makes a person mature. In the two kinds of change that are contrasted here, it seems to me that the authenticity of the Christian willingness to change is clearly evident over against the "cult of movement".

[16] Bonaventure, *De tribus quaestionibus* 13, ed. Quaracci VIII, 336 b. For Bonaventure's overall plan, see J. Ratzinger, *The Theology of History in St. Bonaventure*, 2nd ed. (Chicago: Franciscan Herald Press, 1989).

[17] So it is formulated in Marius Victorinus, *Hymnus* III, 71–73, in this context as a theological, trinitarian adaptation of the Neoplatonic formula for being; cf. Hadot, "Conversio", 1034f. It is clear that one therefore cannot reduce the contrast of Christianity and antiquity—which from the very beginning is also an interdependence—to a simplistic opposition of cyclical vs. linear; cf. Thraede, "Fortschritt", esp. 161f.

Interiority and communion

If one wished to set forth the essential, fundamental certainties of Christian metanoia, one would have to describe, in addition to the interdependence of change and fidelity that I have just tried to explain briefly, two further and similar relationships: the interdependence of interiority and communal character and the interdependence of gift and duty. I am content to make a few general points about each. It seems to me that it is simply wrong when Behm in his meritorious article μετάνοια in the *Theologisches Wörterbuch zum Neuen Testament* lists four possible meanings—"feel remorse", "change one's mind/heart", "repent", and "turn back"—but thinks that only the last meaning applies to Jesus' call and that all the others stray into legalism.[18] It is true, rather, that the whole spectrum of meaning is intended—directed, of course, toward the central idea of turning back. The radical character of Christian conversion requires that it have concreteness as a bodily and communal event: this is the basis for the sacrament of penance as a public ecclesial form of renewed conversion with two foci: real penance (fasting, prayer, and alms)[19] and confession ...

Gift and task—the little way

The interpenetration of gift and task is incomparably clear in the saying of Jesus: "Truly, I say to you, unless you turn and become like children, you will never enter the kingdom of heaven" (Mt 18:3). Behm comments on the passage: "To be a child ... means to be little, to need help and to be receptive to it. Someone who converts becomes little

[18] Marius Victorinus, IV, 994f. and *passim*.
[19] This early Christian triad should be emphasized again in the Church as a concrete proof of repentance.

in God's sight . . . , willing to allow God to work on him. The children of the heavenly Father whom Jesus proclaimed . . . are simply receivers with respect to him. He gives them what they cannot give to themselves. . . . That is true about μετάνοια also. It is God's gift and yet does not cease to be an obligatory demand." [20] This simple center of metanoia, which refers, not to any peremptory extravagances, but rather to our day-by-day patience with God and God's with us, was lovingly exemplified for us toward the end of the nineteenth century by Thérèse of Lisieux: instead of an image of a saint that pointed to heroic virtue and thus mistook the real orientation of Christianity, she followed the "little way"—receiving and approaching him every day. Ida Friederike Görres noted in her diary that she was becoming increasingly convinced that Thérèse by no means stood alone but was only the prototype of a whole movement of little saints around the turn of the century who, without knowing each other and as though by a silent law, grew up unnoticed in the Church and went their way. She then says something about the Irish Jesuit William Doyle, who was killed in 1917 in Ypres and had been born in the same year as Thérèse. Magnificent sayings of his have been recorded, such as this one: "I don't think it would be possible for me to find nourishment for vanity and pride in anything I do . . . any more than an organ grinder is conceited about the beautiful music he produces when he turns the crank. . . . I

---

[20] *ThWNT* 4:998. J. Jeremias gives a beautiful (although somewhat one-sided) interpretation to the verse Matthew 18:3: "'To become children again' means to learn again to say Abba. That brings us to the center of what repentance means. Conversion means learning again to say Abba, placing one's whole trust in the heavenly Father, returning to the Father's house and the Father's embrace. . . . Finally and ultimately, repentance is nothing but entrusting oneself to the grace of God" (*Neutestamentliche Theologie*, vol. 1 [Gütersloh, 1971], 154f.).

feel ashamed when people praise me ... as a piano would
be put to shame if someone congratulated it on the beautiful music that proceeds from its keys." [21] I. F. Görres comments: "Hidden holiness in the Church is already an
important topic. Probably there are dozens of such people
... about whom nobody ever notices anything." [22] And she
asks with some annoyance why people "make such a big
fuss" [23] about Little Thérèse, who after all was only one of
many. "But, obviously, people in fact prefer to accept such
things from a photogenic young girl with a smile, roses,
and a veil. One might wonder whether Thérèse would have
had the same tremendous influence if she had been irremedi-
ably ugly—humpbacked and cross-eyed or something like
that, or if she had lived to an advanced old age." [24]

I think that today there is a sort of answer to this question, a very surprising one. For it seems to me that we have
had the opportunity once again to witness a saint from this
new "wave": John XXIII. Anyone who reads his diary is
disappointed at first and cannot believe that the man of this
old-fashioned seminary asceticism and the great pope of the
renewal were one and the same person. But only when we
see each one in the other have we seen him correctly, have
we seen the whole. These diaries, begun at a time when
Thérèse was still living, are in fact a "little way"—not a
way of greatness. [25] They begin with the average spirituality

---

[21] I. F. Görres, *Zwischen den Zeiten* (Olten-Freiburg, 1960), 271.

[22] Ibid., 273.

[23] Ibid., 270.

[24] Ibid.

[25] The diary begins, characteristically, with a new version, composed by
Roncalli the seminarian, of the "Little Rules" that the spiritual director in
Bergamo had given to his theology students. The Italian editor (L. Capovilla)
comments: "He kept them always by him and constantly observed them,
even when he was pope." John XXIII: *Journal of a Soul*, translated by Dor-
othy White (New York: McGraw-Hill, 1965), 4, n. 1.

of an Italian major seminary in those years, a bit sentim-
mental, a bit narrow, and yet wide open to what is essential. And precisely by following this way, this simplicity, and
this patience in persevering day by day, which can only suc-
ceed through a willingness to change daily—by following
this way, a final spiritual simplicity matured that gives vision
and that caused a little, paunchy old man to become beautiful through a radiance from within. Here everything is
gift, and yet here everything is conversion—metanoia, which
makes Christians and creates saints. "Probably there are dozens of such people", says I. F. Görres—and really we all ought
to try to be among them. For only then are we Christians.

Resurrection of the Dead and the Life of the World to Come

Beyond Death

The question of what lies beyond death was long a dominant theme of Christian thought. Today it has fallen under that suspicion of Platonism which, originating in different ways in Marx and Nietzsche, weighs more and more oppressively on the Christian mind. The "beyond" looks like a flight from the distress and tasks of this world deliberately encouraged and held out as a hope by those holding power here below. Consequently, simply the general attitude to life almost completely blocks access to the question. Furthermore, at a time when the defense of Christian essentials in the face of the "principalities and powers" of this world has become a central concern, the theme may appear secondary even to those who are far from recasting the Christian message into mere social action (or criticism).

There are other barriers as well. The next world is not only beyond the range of our action; it is inaccessible to ratiocination and, therefore, questionable. It looks as though any statement about it cannot be more than a pious conjecture or wish. Finally, even among theologians what was

Translation used by permission of Communio.

apparently quite clear has become very inaccessible; though in this connection it must be taken into account that the kind of theological problems emerging are essentially determined by the shift in general attitude to life as well as by the loss of a philosophy capable of mediating between the facts of revelation and the positive findings of science. The situation is largely characterized by the clash of two positivisms, theological and scientific; this often produces a sort of short-circuit philosophy that does not recognize itself for what it is and, consequently, is all the more self-confident in its assertions. Here, then, we have a wide-ranging task, and one that will also help with the urgent problem of the political and social responsibility of the Christian faith, for even on that subject people will be able to speak on a firmer basis and more effectively if its relation to Christian hope as a whole is clarified. Without an intelligible answer to the question of death, no light can be thrown on the question of man's life and purpose. For this life is in fact marked by death and cannot be planned as though that were not so. And the question of death includes the problem of what is beyond death, the whole problem of nothingness and being.

The resurrection or immortality of the soul antithesis

a. The thesis

Only a few remarks can be offered here on this wide-ranging task. Moreover, they will be essentially theological and consequently nothing more than a first stimulus to further thought. The question has been considerably complicated for Catholics in the course of the last decade by the fact that it was increasingly impossible for them to pay no heed to those Protestant theologians who regard "immortality of the soul" as a thoroughly unbiblical concept. Oscar

Cullmann has been particularly insistent here, and we must recall at least one of his most striking expressions: "If we ask an average Christian, Protestant or Catholic, what the New Testament teaches about the individual lot of man after death, with few exceptions we will receive the answer, 'The immortality of the soul'. In this form, this opinion represents one of the greatest misunderstandings of Christianity." [1] Cullmann speaks in this connection of the incompatibility of the biblical belief in resurrection with the Greek doctrine of immortality. This rejection of the idea of an immortal soul in favor of recognizing the resurrection of the body as alone biblical is of course the result of reading the Bible in the light of a particular hermeneutics. The central content of the latter seems to me to consist in establishing an antithesis between biblical and Greek, which once again includes various themes. It has a long history [2] but in modern theology is more or less consciously regarded as one of the weapons by which Christianity is to be cleared of the imputation of Platonism. In the form in which we find it in Cullmann and the earlier volumes of Kittel's monumental *Theological Dictionary of the New Testament*, it seems to me to be chiefly associated, in the tradition of Protestant thought, with two basic choices: on the one hand, that of banishing philosophy as far as possible from the domain of faith, and, on the other, an extremely radical view of the divine action of grace, that is, a top-down mode of thought that knowingly and decidedly opposes the philosophical

---

[1] O. Cullmann, *Unsterblichkeit der Seele und Auferstehung der Toten* (1956), 19; English trans., *The Immortality of the Soul, or the Resurrection of the Dead* (1958).

[2] On the history of the question, cf. A. Grillmeier, "Hellenisierung und Judaisierung des Christentums als Deuteprinzipien der Geschichte des kirchlichen Dogmas", *Scholastik* 33 (1958): 321–55, 528–58. The influence and background of the idea in recent theology would need a whole study to themselves.

schema of ascent.[3] The terms "soul" and "immortality" are
suspect by the mere fact that they are the product of philosophical reflection; while the affirmation of an immortality of the soul flowing from man's essential constitution
appears to express something naturally belonging to man as
opposed to raising from the dead, which can only be effected
by God, in other words, by sheer grace. As a result, not
only the idea of immortality but also that of "soul" itself
falls under the suspicion of Platonism and has to make way
for a doctrine of man as a totality that knows no such distinction in man.

b. The problems

At this point we also see the connection with the modern
mentality or attitude to life (and the trend of modern scientific anthropology). There is a rediscovery, a new feeling
for the human body; science has everywhere found confirmation of the unity of man and his complete indivisibility.
This is precisely what corresponds to the fundamental tenor
of biblical thought and contradicts the dualism that with some
justification can be attributed to Platonism.[4] But if this gets
rid of one difficulty, that of Platonism, another no less grave
takes its place. For now one would have to say that if the
immortality of the soul as a substance independent of the

[3] The classical presentation of an antithesis between the ascent and descent
schemas is that of A. Nygren, *Eros und Agape: Gestaltwandlungen der christli-
chen Liebe* (1930, 1937). For a discussion of this, cf. J. Pieper, *Über die Liebe*
(Munich, 1972), 92–106; valuable indications (in the sense of a Christian
rehabilitation of Eros) in H. de Lubac, *History and Spirit*, trans. Anne Englund
Nash and Juvenal Merriell of the Oratory (San Francisco: Ignatius Press, 2007),
270–72.

[4] "Platonism" has sunk here to a mere catchword that has no longer anything to do with the historical reality of Platonic philosophy, the great political relevance of which has recently been forcefully brought out by U. Duchrow,
Christenheit und Weltverantwortung (Stuttgart, 1970), 61–80.

body contradicts the Bible as well as modern knowledge, what about the raising of the dead? If this is not to be relegated into the sphere of the purely miraculous, but is to be thought of in reasonable terms, even greater difficulties arise. Are we to think of it happening for everyone "on the Last Day"? If so, what lies in between? A sleep of the soul? Or total death? And if so, who exactly can be raised from the dead? What constitutes the identity between dead and resurrected if complete nonbeing intervenes? And what is resurrected? The doctrine of man as a totality seems to demand a body and, basically, can recognize only a body as bearer of identity (if the soul is completely rejected); but how is human identity to be maintained in the body alone? How can man's restoration be intelligibly conceived at all? How are we to picture the life and mode of existence of those raised from the dead? Is it obvious that without rational thought along the logical lines of the biblical statements, that is to say, philosophical mediation (without "hermeneutics"), no further advance can be made. But in that case, it can no longer be forbidden to ask whether something like the concept of the soul is not needed after all as a hermeneutical connecting link, whether it is not, in fact, suggested by the data themselves, even if the latter take reflection in this direction no farther than a step or two.

For the moment, however, let us continue to establish the state of the question. It was at once widely recognized that a general postponement of the solution of the problem of death to the "end of time" is unsatisfactory and, together with the question of the intermediate state and the preservation of identity, involves a further series of practically insoluble problems. Consequently, a philosophy of time is in many cases introduced here, of the kind, for example, that was worked out by Karl Barth in his early days, drawing on Ernst Troeltsch in regard to the problem of eschatology.

Troeltsch had expressed the idea that the Last Things really
stand in no relation to time.[5] To say that they will come
"at the end of time", "after our time" is, he claims, merely
a makeshift way of speaking in such terms as our time-
bound minds can find. In reality, the otherness of the
Eschaton is simply incommensurable with our time. Consequently, it is argued, one might say that every wave of the
sea of time breaks in the same way on the shore of eternity.
The early Barth could accordingly write that to wait for
the parousia is equivalent to "taking our actual situation in
life as seriously as it really is". Similarly, the parousia is identical with the resurrection, which is not a phenomenon in
time but an emanation of eternity, and symbolizes what is
the ultimate in the metaphysical sense.[6] Here the question
inescapably arises of the actual real content of such formulations. Do they turn eschatology into a rather more elaborate formulation of men's day-to-day responsibilities? Or
what do they actually state?

In Catholic theology, ideas from this philosophy of time
and eternity gained increased acceptance in connection with
the discussion of the dogma of Mary's bodily Assumption
into heavenly glory. Here a raising from the dead that had
already taken place was explicitly affirmed, even if only
directly in regard to one human being, the Mother of the
Lord. Nevertheless, this raised quite generally the question
of what constitutes the resurrection of the body and its relation to time. And so this dogma appeared, in the perspective of the discussions that had been going on, as a downright

---

[5] I am following here the account given by F. Holmström, *Das eschatolo-
gische Denken der Gegenwart* (Gütersloh, 1937); on Troeltsch, cf. 131ff. Cf.
also F. M. Braun, *Neues Licht auf die Kirche* (Einsiedeln and Cologne, 1946),
93–132.

[6] K. Barth, *Der Römerbrief*, 2nd ed. (Munich, 1922), 240ff.; English trans.,
1933. Cf. Braun, *Neues Licht*, 113f.

challenge to correct a purely linear representation of the end of time and, instead, to think of the Last Things, death, and resurrection as coextensive with time.[7] This made it possible to remove the particular stumbling block of this dogma, which could now be regarded simply as the paradigm case of the fundamental correlation of time and eternity; similarly, eschatological problems can be clarified by a new understanding of what "end" means in relation to time. The view gained wide acceptance that each man's death is entry into the wholly other, into what is not time but eternity. Eternity does not come *after* time (that would mean it was itself in time); it is time's counterpart, ever present and contemporaneous with it. Consequently, dying in each case means dying into eternity, into the "end of time", into the total Eschaton, into the already present resurrection and fulfillment. Just as the spatial conception of the beyond as a sort of upper story of the world was only slowly and not without opposition replaced by a personal and metaphysical view, so in the same way a temporal conception of it as an end coming "after" world-time must be got rid of. For this view is, we are told, no less naive and misses no less radically the essential structure of the time–eternity relation.

This philosophy of time and eternity abandons the attempt to be satisfied with a simple Bible positivism, and by reflection on the different levels of reality some progress is undoubtedly achieved. At the same time, the idea of the resurrection of the dead is considerably modified (unfortunately, for the most part, without sufficient consideration). For the dead laid in the earthly grave is simultaneously said to be already risen on the other side of the line of time.

---

[7] One of the first attempts to interpret the dogma of the Assumption in this way was that of O. Karrer, "Über unsterbliche Seele und Auferstehung", *Anima* 11 (1953): 332–36.

What does that mean? Is there, after all, a human existence separable from the body? Something like the "soul", in fact? Or what kind of concept of time is it that seems to make it possible to think of man as both risen and as lying in the grave? Either way, further questions are inescapable.

In search of new answers

a. Physical time—human time—eternity

Let us continue with the problem of time. The distinction between time and eternity, which has been adopted as a sort of magic key to solve the problem, makes possible some progress, as we have noted, as compared with an unanalyzed linear extension in which an end that as such is no longer time is, nevertheless, simply located "after" time and so turned into time. But it remains far behind the stage of reflection reached by Augustine and pursued in the Middle Ages in various forms. Augustine's fundamental insight in his considerations on human memory consists in the distinction he draws between physical time and time as humanly experienced. The latter in fact offers a model on which eternity can at least be thought about, but it is not eternity. Physical time denotes the successive moments of a process of movement that can be ascertained and dated by reference to a particular parameter (sun or moon, for example). Its essential features are uniformity and irrevocability. The movement in question (revolution of a body, and so on) can be repeated, yet the movement that has once taken place is irrevocably past and as such can only be verified as the date when something did happen. In short, physical time might be defined as the measurable course of corporeal movement. Now man, because corporeal, is tied to physical time. The stages of his bodily and therefore, indirectly, of his mental existence can be fitted into the general course of movement of bodies and dated in days and years by the course of the sun. But it is obvious that man's personal experience is not wholly identical with measurable corporeal movement. While it is true that even human processes of intellectual decision are connected with the body and to that extent, as we have said, can be dated indirectly, in themselves they are something different from corporeal movement and to that extent transcend the measures of physical time. What is "present" for each human being is determined, not solely by the calendar, but much more by his mental attention, the section of reality he grasps as present, as effectively Now. To this present belong his hopes and fears, that is, what is chronologically future, as well as his fidelity and gratitude, in other words, what is chronologically past. "The present" in this sense is a strictly human phenomenon, differing from one human being to another (in different human beings, different present times meet); physical time has only moments. Augustine tried to designate this specifically human phenomenon by the term "memory". Memory unites a segment, determined by my vital decisions, from the chronological past and future to my human present. This human time does not possess either the uniformity or the absolute irrevocability of the physical time process. Human acts cannot be repeated with their unique character as a particular physical movement can; on the other hand, they do not simply pass away, but "remain". Love in its very essence endures; truth, once discovered, abides; my human experiences are a real part of my living self. Present consciousness, which is able to summon what is past into the present of recollection, thus makes possible some notion of what "eternity" is: pure *memoria* bearing the whole changing movement of the world in the all-inclusive present of the creative mind, yet comprehending each detail exactly as it is at its own chronological point.

If we apply this to our previous considerations, the weakness of the time and eternity philosophy described above appears to me to be that it presents a single alternative: physical time or pure eternity; moreover, it conceives the latter quite negatively as the non-temporal. Death, then, appears simply as the change from physical time to eternity. But this overlooks precisely the specifically human element. Consequently, the answer turns out to be quite insufficient. For if one were rigorously to follow up the idea that beyond death a pure Now prevails, that resurrection, end of the world, and Last Judgment are already present, because there is no time there, this would mean that in each instance men would enter into the whole of completed history and into the complete timelessness that prevails there, thus finding there all those people who think they are still living in the course of time or in general still belong to the future. This absurd consequence inescapably follows from the conception in question. It would also mean that, viewed from the other side, history would be an empty spectacle in which people think they are striving and struggling, whereas simultaneously in "eternity", in the already ever present Now, everything is long since decided. A shoddy "Platonism", such as Plato and the Platonists never knew, would thus result from thinking in terms of a sole antithesis between physical time and eternity. In contrast to this, a correct description of what happens at death would have to say, for example, that specifically human time is detached here from its physical chronological context and thereby receives a definitive character. But that means that the two sides of man and history do not stand to one another in a relation of simple succession, but are also not absolutely incommensurable. Which also means that the unfolding history of the world and its definitive theo-logical future most certainly stand in a real relation to one another, that the activity of the one is not at all a matter of no account to the genesis of the other. The common future of the creation, of which faith speaks, and the future of the world toward which our activity is directed cannot be calculated in terms of one another, but they are nonetheless inseparable.

Rehabilitation of the soul

There remains the question of the soul. It cannot be denied that this term was accepted with some hesitation into Christian tradition, even though the transition of biblical faith into the domain of Greek thought was prepared and in part carried out much earlier than the harsh antithesis to which we referred earlier would suggest. I need only recall that intertestamental Judaism already had very elaborate conceptions of the life and conditions of men after death, and these for a very long time gave their stamp to the mental world of the ancient Church and, even in Augustine, were still exercising more influence than Plato's schemata.[8] The prayer of the Roman Canon that the dead may have a place of light, peace, and refreshment (= of running water) preserves to this day an expression from that world of Jewish beliefs that survived in the Church. Continuity of that kind is precisely what provides an indication on how to read the New Testament correctly in this question. The apostolic preaching presupposes in principle that Israel's faith is its own, with, of course, the one decisive proviso that it must

[8] On the development of the doctrine of the "intermediate state" in the ancient Church, cf. in particular A. Stuiber, *Refrigerium interim* (Bonn, 1957); J. Fischer, *Studien zum Todesgedanken in der alten Kirche* (Munich, 1954). There is a good collection of materials in Y. Trémel, "Der Mensch zwischen Tod und Auferstehung nach dem Neuen Testament", *Anima* 11 (1953): 313–31.

be viewed and lived in its entirety with Christ as basis and
in relation to Christ; in him it receives a new center, and
this slowly pervaded its various elements. But this process
of reshaping the various elements through faith in Christ
took time, proceeded slowly. What difference it made to
particular elements of Jewish belief that they had now to be
read in relation to Christ did not necessarily have to be
decided immediately except in central matters. Consequently, for a very long time eschatology remained, so to
speak, in a largely Jewish condition, but this testifies in fact
to the continuity of the ancient Church with the original
Jewish Christian community. The new emphasis consists in
the fact that Jesus Christ is proclaimed as having already
risen. The real point of reference of immortality is less some
coming time than the living Lord now. Thus Paul gave a
radically christological and personal interpretation of the late
Jewish doctrine of the intermediate realms in the words,
"to be dissolved and be with Christ" (Phil 1:23). The Lord
is where our indestructible life is, and there is no need to
ask questions about or seek any other place. In the Synoptic Gospels, two sayings of Jesus have been preserved in
more archaic formulations of a more Jewish coloring. In
the context of the story of Lazarus at Luke 16:19–29, mention is made of Abraham's bosom as the place of salvation,
contrasted with the place of torment, separated from it by
an unbridgeable abyss. The good thief receives the answer
from the dying Lord, "This day you will be with me in
Paradise" (Lk 23:43).[9] This recalls the late Jewish theology
of martyrdom also reechoed in the account of the first Christian martyrdom: "Lord Jesus, receive my spirit" is Stephen's
dying prayer (Acts 7:59). Already in the words to the good
thief, "with me" introduces a christological nuance to the

---

[9] Cf. J. Jeremias, "παράδεισος," in *ThWNT*, 5:763–71, esp. 768f.

idea of Paradise, and in the prayer of the Christian martyr, the Lord himself is the Paradise into which the dying man knows his life is taken up. No longer the bosom of the patriarch Abraham is the place of shelter for the believer's existence, but the risen Lord in whom those who are his own live.

Thus, in relation to the risen Lord, there was now an awareness of a life bestowed on men even in the death of the body and before the final accomplishment of the world's future. It was, accordingly, realized that there is a human continuity that extends beyond the identity of man's corporeal existence, even though he is himself in his body a single indivisible creature. How was this factor of continuity and identity to be thought of? Even in earthly life, it is more than the sum of the material parts of man (which, of course, change even during his earthly life), and its real significance only really becomes apparent in the possibility of an existence beyond death. Greek had the term "soul" to offer, which for that matter here and there in the New Testament had already carried the meaning of this factor of identity transcending corporeality.[10] Of course, this expression had the drawback of being associated with a dualistic world view and was, therefore, dangerous and could not be used without clarification. But that was fundamentally the case with all words, even the word "God". The Greek "God" was not at all the same as the biblical Yahweh, the Father of Jesus Christ, so that the common use of the name "God" involved a no less serious possible danger. On the other hand, it must not be forgotten that the words of

[10] J. Schmid, "Der Begriff der Seele im Neuen Testament", in *Einsicht und Glaube*, ed. J. Ratzinger and H. Fries, 2nd ed., 128–48 (Freiburg, 1963), minimizes this as far as he can but cannot eliminate it entirely. Cf. also, on the different levels of meaning, P. van Imschoot, "Seele", in *Bibellexikon*, ed. H. Haag, 2nd ed., 1567f. (Einsiedeln, 1968).

the Bible themselves did not fall from heaven, but were turned into ways of expressing faith by molding and clarifying words taken from Israel's religious and secular environment. It is possible to observe how hesitantly and gradually that reshaping took place, and not without relapses, and never actually ceased. Except by the slow transformation of words and thoughts that man has discovered during history, it is impossible to preach the faith at all. To that extent, therefore, the dualist origin of the term "soul" says something about the danger but nothing about the impossibility in principle of using it. More recent studies have conclusively shown how intensively Christian thought, especially at the height of the Middle Ages, endeavored to achieve the necessary purification and transformation of the concept.[11] Unfortunately it is impossible to go into details, but it could be shown that the doctrine of the immortality of the soul as Thomas Aquinas formulated it represents something radically new in comparison with the immortality doctrines of antiquity. Aristotle, of whom Aquinas makes use in his own thinking, actually denies that the *forma corporis* (the integrative force of the body) is immortal, just as he denies that the immortal element (the *intellectus agens*) belongs to the individual as such. Similarly, Plato would never have admitted that the "immortal soul" is so linked to the body, belongs to it in such a way and is so one with it, that it must be called its "form" and cannot subsist except in closest relation to it.

---

[11] Cf. the unpublished Bochum thesis of T. Schneider, *Die Einheit des Menschen: Die anthropologische Formel "Anima forma corporis" im sogennanten Korrektorienstreit und bei Petrus Johannis Olivi: Ein Beitrag zur Vorgeschichte des Konzils von Vienne*. Cf. also the unpublished Regensburg thesis of H.J. Weber, *Die Lehre von der Auferstehung der Toten in den Haupttraktaten der scholastischen Theologie von Alexander von Hales zu Duns Scotus*. Cf. also the references given by J. Pieper, "Tod und Unsterblichkeit", *Catholica* 13 (1953): 81–100.

There is no doubt, of course, that a dualistic element has repeatedly imposed itself to a considerable extent on the public mind. To that extent, a new endeavor to purify the concept or even to seek to formulate it better is certainly not out of place. But the reality itself cannot be bypassed, certainly not if the message of the New Testament is to be preserved without diminution. Perhaps some light can be had from another side on what is meant. Talk of the immortal soul has a suspicious ring about it today because people have the impression it refers to an objectifying metaphysics of substance, whereas in contrast to this a dialogical, personal concept is regarded as more appropriate. Accordingly, the question of what actually makes man immortal appears to call for a different kind of answer. It is for that matter identical with the question of what is distinctive and specific in man, what makes man human. In a dialogical conception, the answer would be that this distinctive feature lies in his capacity for God, in the fact that he is addressed by God and is in principle called upon to respond. Anyone who speaks with God does not die. God's love gives eternity.[12] But this thought differs from the true sense of an authentic concept of the "soul" only in mode of formulation and approach. Augustine deduced man's immortality from his capacity for truth. Aquinas follows him in this: Anyone who has commerce with truth shares in its indestructibility.[13] Nowadays we should lay more emphasis on the dialogue of mutual love, but the line of

[12] I tried to formulate the idea of immortality on these lines in my *Introduction to Christianity*, trans. J. R. Foster, rev. ed. (San Francisco: Ignatius Press, 2004), 301–10, esp.

[13] Cf. references in Pieper, "Tod und Unsterblichkeit", 96f.; Augustine, *Solil.* 2, 19 (PL 32, 901); Aquinas, *S. Th.* I, q. 62, a 2 ad 3 (here applied to the angels: "... ex hoc quod habent naturam per quam sunt capaces veritatis, sunt incorruptibiles").

thought is the same. But that means that "soul" and "capacity for truth" or "to be called to indestructible dialogue with eternal truth and love" are all expressions for one and the same thing. Soul is not an occult entity that one *has*, a partial substance hidden somewhere in a human being; it is the dynamism of an unlimited openness, which at the same time means participation in infinity, in the eternal. Conversely, however, it is also the case that the dynamic character of human personal life, the thirst for truth and indestructible love, is not a disconnected, merely factual succession, but, most fragile as that dynamism is, it is also the most authentic and enduring reality. This dynamism is substance, and this substance is dynamism. This fundamental, enduring, and essential human reality is recalled to mind by the term "soul". This presupposes, of course, that we do not think of substance from below, in terms of "mass" (which in any case is itself becoming more problematic), but from above, in terms of the dynamism of mental activity, and that we cease to regard solid "mass" as what is most certainly real—the contrary is the case.

A radio program under the title "Is the soul immortal?" was recently introduced with the remark that the question—if unexpanded and left without comment—sounds absurd and even "obscene". Now there is in fact a kind of shame that ought to impel us not to rob great things of their dignity by frivolous use. To that extent, everyday misuse of elevated language can in fact become in a certain sense "obscene", and it cannot be denied that there have been cases of this in everyday Christian language. On the other hand, in an age in which the shame that ought to protect the dignity and grandeur of the human body is increasingly scorned, things should not be allowed to come to such a pitch that man is ashamed of his spirit, his "soul", in a way that threatens to degenerate into a total (and very ominous) taboo. It seems to me that it is high time theology set about rehabilitating the taboo concepts of "immortality" and the "soul". Certainly they raise problems, and the shock of the last few years may prove to have been salutary or even necessary. It will no longer be possible to use the words as simply and unthinkingly as formerly. But simply to outlaw them is at bottom just as naive and bars access to the whole problem. It makes no difference to object that they go beyond biblical terminology. Anyone who regards that as putting an end to the matter would be denying the whole problem of hermeneutics, the whole function of reflective mediation.

Belief in immortality and secular responsibility

The problem remains: What is the point of it all? The biblical question, "What does it profit a man if he gain the whole world but suffers the loss of his own soul?" appears nowadays to be inverted into the question of what it profits a man to gain his whole soul if the world is not served thereby. A lot might be said on this; perhaps this kind of inversion of the question represents the main problem of Christian life today. In accordance with the fragmentary character of these reflections, only a suggestion or two can be attempted, certainly inadequate, but enough perhaps to help open up a line of thought. As is well known, Dietrich Bonhoeffer once formulated the thought that the believer today must live *quasi Deus non daretur*—as though God did not exist. I fully agree with what this saying is intended to express, namely, that we must avoid an egotistical and primitive notion of God that misuses him as a stopgap in our earthly failure. Nevertheless, I think that for the conduct of life it would be more appropriate to suggest the opposite. Even the skeptic and the atheist should live *quasi Deus daretur*—as though God really existed.

What does that mean? To live as though God existed
means to live as though one had an unlimited responsibility; as though justice and truth were not only programs,
but a living existent power to which one had to render an
account; as though what one did now would not disappear like a drop in the ocean, but was of lasting, even
permanent consequence. To act as though God existed
would also mean to act as though the human being next
to me were not just some chance product of nature, of no
great ultimate importance, but an embodied thought of
God, an image of the Creator whom God knows and loves.
That would mean acting as though each human being were
destined for eternity and as though each were my brother
because created by the same God. To act *quasi Deus daretur*, as though God existed, seems to me to be the only
meaningful replacement for Kant's categorical imperative
in an age when the conditions required for its application
have been destroyed. Kant had tried to solve the ethical
problem by the simple maxim: Act in such a way that the
maxim of your conduct could at all times serve as a law
for all. The idea is that by this procedure in practice one
will always hit on the good. What can be generalized can
be justified in relation to the whole. This at first very clear
solution is in fact only practicable as long as people remain
more or less agreed about *what* can be generalized and what
forms of action are appropriate as general laws. Kant's imperative, therefore, presupposes a society in which a definite
value structure exists and in which people are to some
degree certain what serves the well-being of the whole
and what does not. But this is precisely what we have
become so disunited about today in a way that Kant could
not have imagined. According to what theory of society is
held, exact contraries will be regarded as a possible general
law. The point of reference that provided the basis of Kant's

thought, namely universality, human society, is too uncertain for human action to be securely built on it alone.

To act as though God existed—anyone who tries this reaches without much further reflection the kernel of belief in the immortality of the soul. Even if perhaps he can never get farther than the "as if" and remains a life-long questioner, he has accepted what is really at issue much more than someone who affirms immortality as a formula but lives as though there were no one but himself. An important point emerges here that has not been mentioned so far: The real import of Christian belief in the immortality of the soul is not to posit some theory or other about things we can know nothing about and subsequently declare to be certain; it makes a statement about the standards and scope of human life. It is intended to inculcate that man is never a means but always an end in himself. It seeks to impress on the mind the reality of values, especially those of justice and truth, that are not mere abstract goals but life and life-giving. To that extent, it is a thoroughly practical statement. A decision about the status and dignity of human life.

Once this has been said, we can go a step farther. Human life cannot ultimately be based on an "as if". That may work quite well with an individual if the "as if" has powerful enough support; it may suffice on long stretches of human life in which theoretical solutions are suspended and people simply push on in the darkness. But it cannot be the fundamental form of human personal existence as such. If it is the case that human existence can actually be constructed on the basis of this "as if", this implies something about the validity and reality of the hypothesis. The same thing may be approached from another angle. Anyone who patiently trusts to this "as if", taking it constantly as the maxim of his life, can see that he is not living by a fiction, that what he at first adopted as a hypothesis is true, the authentic truth about man and reality itself.[14]

Truth and justice are not simply ideas, they *are*. In other words, God *is*. This, however, basically implies immortality. For God is a God of the living. The idea of God, to my mind, already includes that of man's immortality. For a creature who is looked upon and loved by him who is eternity has thereby a share in eternity. How exactly one is to formulate this, or even how one is to think it, are *ultimately* secondary, though by no means unimportant, questions. All the concepts we employ—and so also the affirmation of the immortality of the *soul*—are in the last resort mere aids to thought (partly, of course, irreplaceable) with which we try on the basis of various anthropological models to define the whole more concretely. Such conceptual advances are unquestionably necessary for us to see more clearly and firmly maintain the demands and responsibility of rational thought. But they are not the essential. And, above all, there is no question at all of obtaining descriptions of the beyond, thus extending the range of our vain curiosity. In essence, the confession of belief in immortality is nothing else than a profession of faith that God really exists. It is a statement about God, and precisely for that reason it is a statement about man who is to find in it the way and manner of his personal life.

[14] This section was delivered in the course of the above-mentioned broadcast from Radio Free Berlin. The producers (L. Dilzen and H. Wöller) commented that "to save the principle of life which we call 'soul'", I had "demanded an intellectual effort and the capacity for rational abstraction, which (was) rewarded by belief in the possibility of eternal existence". It would be impossible to imagine a more absurd misinterpretation of what I said. I was simply trying to bring out the reference to practice which is inherent in religious cognition and which is impossible without a context of experience.

The Church's Credo

Why I Am Still in the Church[1]

Today there are many and contradictory reasons not to be in the Church any more. It is no longer only the people to whom the Church's faith has become strange and to whom the Church seems too backward, too medieval, too hostile to the world and to life who turn their back on the Church, but also the people who loved the Church's historical form, her liturgy, her timelessness, and the reflection of the eternal in her. It seems to them that the Church is intent on betraying what is essential to her, that she is selling herself to current trends and thus losing her soul: they are disillusioned like a lover who experiences the betrayal of a great love and has to make a serious attempt to turn his back on it.

Conversely, however, there are also quite contradictory reasons to stay in the Church: the ones who remain are not

Translated by Michael J. Miller.

[1] Given the parameters of a lecture and the special nature of the theme assigned to me, it goes without saying that it was not possible to attempt a comprehensive presentation of the objective reasons for being in the Church. I had to be content with fitting together, as though in a mosaic, a few remarks about a decision that is ultimately my own personal responsibility, which nonetheless can perhaps make evident in their own way something of an objective law.

only those who steadfastly adhere to their faith in her mission or those who are unwilling to sever their ties to a dear old habit (even though they make little use of that habit). Also remaining in the Church today, with the greatest insistence, are those who reject her entire historical nature and passionately oppose the content that her officials try to give to her or uphold. Although they want to do away with what the Church was and is, they are determined not to be ousted, so that they can make of her what, in their opinion, she is supposed to become.

Preliminary reflection on the situation of the Church

All this, however, produces a veritable Tower of Babel within the Church: not only are the reasons pro and con mixed up in the strangest ways, but it seems hardly possible any more to reach an understanding. Above all: mistrust is on parade, because being in the Church has lost its clear meaning, and in the resulting ambiguity no one dares to trust the other's honesty. Romano Guardini's hopeful assessment, written in 1921, seems to have turned into its opposite: "A momentous process has begun: the Church is awakening in souls." Today it seems that the saying should read conversely: indeed, a momentous process is taking place—the Church is being extinguished in souls and is collapsing in communities. In the midst of a world that is striving for unity, the Church is crumbling into nationalistic resentment, in the disparagement of what is foreign, in the glorification of what is one's own. Between the managers of worldliness and the reactionaries who cling all too much to externals and to what merely has been, between a disregard for tradition and a positivistic building upon the letter of the law, there seems to be no middle ground—public opinion implacably assigns each to his place; it needs clear labels and cannot be bothered about nuances. Anyone who is not for progress is against it; one has to be either a conservative or a progressive. Of course the reality, thank God, is different: in silence and as yet almost without a spokesman, there are meanwhile, even today, simple believers, who even in this hour of confusion carry out the real task of the Church: worship and the patience of everyday life, nourished by the Word of God. But they do not fit into the desired picture, and so they remain for the most part silent—this true Church, while not invisible, is nevertheless hidden deep beneath the doings of men.

This gives us a preliminary hint about the background for the question that arises today: Why do I still stay in the Church? If we are to answer it meaningfully, we must first analyze in greater depth this background, which because of that little word "today" is directly concerned with our topic, and we must now go beyond observation to inquire into the reasons for it.

How could this remarkable Tower of Babel situation come about just when we were hoping to have a new Pentecost? How is it possible that at the very moment when the Council seemed to have gathered in the mature harvest from the awakening of the last decades, the result was suddenly a terrible emptiness instead of a wealth of fulfillment? How could it happen that this great new movement aimed at unity should produce disintegration? I would like to try, first, to answer with a comparison, which at the same time can reveal the task we have before us and, thereby, suggest the reasons that, despite all that is negative, continue to make an affirmative possible. It seems that in all our efforts to understand the Church—which finally at the Council became an active struggle over her, a work being done concretely on the Church—we got so close to this same Church that now we no longer manage to perceive the whole. We can no longer see the city for the houses, the forest for the trees. The situation into which science has so often led us with regard to reality seems to have come about now with respect to the Church as well. We see the particular detail with such excessive precision that it becomes impossible for us to perceive the whole. And just as in science, so too here: the gain in exactitude means a loss in truth. However indisputably correct everything is that the microscope shows us when we look at a piece of a tree under it, it can still, at the same time, conceal the truth if it causes us to forget that the particular detail is not just the particular but has its existence within the whole, which cannot be put under the microscope and yet is true, truer than the isolated detail.

Let us say things now without metaphor. The contemporary perspective has further modified our view of the Church: in practice, we see the Church now exclusively under the aspect of feasibility, what we can make out of her. The intensive effort for reform in the Church finally caused everything else to be forgotten; to us today she is only a structure that we can change, which confronts us with the question of what we ought to change so as to make her "more efficient" for whatever purposes the individual may have in mind. In the popular mentality, the idea of reform has to a great extent degenerated into this inquiry and thus has been robbed of its essence. For reform, in the original sense, is a spiritual process, quite closely related to conversion and in this sense part of the core of Christianity: only through conversion does one become a Christian: that is true for the individual throughout his lifetime, and it is true for the Church throughout history. She, too, lives as Church by the fact that she converts again and again to the Lord, turns away from her stubborn insistence on what is her own, on mere habit, which, although comforting, can so easily be contrary to the truth. But when reform is separated from this context, from the drudgery of conversion, and salvation is now expected solely from change in other people, from new forms and new structures and more and more adaptations to the times, then many useful things may happen, but as a whole the Church becomes a caricature of herself. Basically, such reform can affect only the unimportant, secondary things in the Church; no wonder the Church herself eventually appears to be something secondary to such reformers! If we reflect on that, then we can also understand the paradox that seems to have resulted from present-day efforts at renewal: the effort to relax rigid structures, to correct forms of ecclesiastical ministry that originated in the Middle Ages or even more in the era of absolutism and to free the Church from such accretions for the sake of simpler service according to the spirit of the Gospel—this effort has in fact led to an overestimation of the ministerial element of the Church that is almost unprecedented in her history. Granted, the institutions and ministries in the Church are criticized more radically today than ever before, but they also absorb our attention more exclusively than they did formerly: quite a few people suppose that the Church today consists of those things alone. The question about the Church, then, is completely taken up by the battle for her institutions: one does not want to allow such an elaborate apparatus to go unused, yet one finds it quite impractical for the new purposes that are assigned to it.

Behind this, the next topic, the crucial one, becomes visible: the crisis of faith, which is the real core of the process. The sociological radius of Church still extends far beyond the circle of actual believers, and through this institutionalized falsehood she is profoundly alienated from her true nature. The publicity effect of the Council and the apparent possibility of a rapprochement between belief and unbelief, which the news coverage almost inevitably feigned, radicalized this alienation to the extreme: the applause for the Council came in part from those who had no intention whatsoever to become believers themselves, as Christian tradition understands it, but rather greeted the "progress" the Church was making toward their own stance as a confirmation of their way. At the same time, of course, also within the Church, herself, the faith was in a tense state of agitation. The problem of historical transmission causes the old Creed to enter into an indistinct twilight in which the outlines of things blur; the claims of the natural sciences, or rather of what is considered to be the modern world view, do their part in aggravating this process. The boundaries between interpretation and denial become increasingly unrecognizable, precisely at the heart of the matter: What does "risen from the dead" really mean? Who believes, who interprets, who denies? And as a result of the debate about the limits of interpretation, the face of God noticeably disappears. "The death of God" is a very real process, which today reaches deep into the interior of the Church. God is dying in Christendom, so it seems. For wherever resurrection becomes a commissioning event that is perceived in outmoded imagery, God is not at work. Does he act at all? That is the question that follows hard on the heels of such ingenious speculation. But who wants to be so reactionary as to insist on a realistic "He is risen"? Thus what others necessarily consider unbelief is for some progress, and what was hitherto unthinkable becomes normal: that men who long ago abandoned the Church's Creed can in good conscience regard themselves as the truly progressive Christians. For them, however, the only standard by which to measure the Church is the expediency with which she functions; of course the question remains as to what is expedient and for what purpose the whole thing is really supposed to be functioning. To critique society, to aid international development, to foment revolution? Or to lead congregational celebrations? In any case, one must start over from the ground up, because the Church was not originally made for all that and in her present form she probably does not really function very well for those purposes. Thus the uneasiness increases among believers and unbelievers. The domestic rights that unbelief has acquired in the Church make the situation seem increasingly intolerable for both groups; above all, through these developments the reform program has tragically drifted into an odd ambiguity for which many people no longer see any solution.

Now naturally one can say: But that is not the whole situation we are facing. Indeed, there have also been so many positive developments in recent years that simply cannot be ignored—the new accessibility of the liturgy, the heightened awareness of social problems, better understanding among separated Christians, the dismantling of a lot of fears that had grown out of a false belief in the letter of the law, and much more. That is true, and it should not be belittled. But it is not characteristic of the "prevailing weather system" in the Church today (if I may put it that way). On the contrary, all this, too, has meanwhile been drawn into the shady area that has resulted from the blurring of the boundaries between belief and unbelief. Only initially did the result of this blurring seem to be liberating. Today it is clear that despite all the existing signs of hope, this process has produced, not a modern Church, but, rather, a deeply divided Church that has become questionable all around. Let us put it quite bluntly: The First Vatican Council had described the Church as "signum levatum in nationes" (a signal flag raised for the nations), as the great eschatological banner visible from afar that calls people together and unites them. It was (as the Council in 1870 supposed) the ensign for which Isaiah hoped (11:12), visible from afar, which everyone could recognize and which unambiguously showed the way to all: with her marvelous propagation, her sublime holiness, her fruitfulness in all good works, and her unshakable stability, she was the genuine miracle of Christianity, its constant authentication in the sight of history, replacing all other signs and wonders.[2] Today all this seems to have turned into the opposite: not marvelous propagation, but a parochial, stagnant club that was incapable of surpassing in earnest the limits of the European or the medieval mind; not sublime holiness, but, rather, a compendium of all human offenses, defiled and humiliated by a history that did not miss out on a single scandal, from persecutions of heretics and witch hunts, from the persecution of the Jews and the enslavements of consciences to self-dogmatization and rebellion against scientific evidence, so that anyone who belongs to this history can only cover his head in shame; and finally, not stability, but, rather, being swept along by all the currents of history, by colonialism and nationalism, and even now about to make an arrangement with Marxism and, if possible, even to be largely identified with it. . . . Thus the Church appears to be, not a sign summoning us to faith, but, rather, the chief obstacle to accepting it.

If there is to be a true theology of the Church now, it seems that it can only consist of taking away her theological attributes and regarding and discussing her as something purely political. The Church herself seems to be no longer a reality of the faith but a quite accidental, albeit for many people indispensable, organization of believers, which ought to be restructured as quickly as possible according to the latest findings of sociology. Trust is good, but

---

[2] Denzinger-Schönmetzer, *Enchiridion Symbolorum*, 32nd ed. (Freiburg, 1963), nos. 3013f.

verification [*Kontrolle*] is better—after all the disappoint-
ments, this is now the slogan with regard to ecclesiastical
ministry. The sacramental principle is no longer intelligible; democratic checks and balances seem now to be the
only reliable alternative:[3] finally, even the Holy Spirit is
much too intangible. Anyone who is not afraid to look at
the past knows, of course, that the humiliations of history
were based precisely on following this path: man managed
to seize power and considered his accomplishments to be
the only real thing.

An image for the nature of the Church

A Church that is viewed only politically, contrary to her
entire history and her distinctive nature, makes no sense,
and a merely political decision to remain in the Church is
dishonest, even if it chants the slogan of honesty. But then,
given the present situation, how can one justify staying in
the Church? To put it differently: The decision in favor of
the Church must be a spiritual decision if it is to have any
meaning—but how can such a spiritual decision be justified? Once again I would like to give a preliminary answer
in the form of a metaphor and, to do so, will refer back to
the statement offered initially to depict the situation. We
had said that in tampering with the Church we have come
so close to her that our perception of the whole is gone.
This thought can be expanded if we make use of an image
that the Church Fathers found in their symbolic meditation on the Church and the world. They explained that in

[3] There may be some justification for such a demand, and to a large extent
it may be quite compatible with the sacramentally defined form of Church
leadership; this point is developed, with the necessary distinctions, in: J. Ratzinger and H. Maier, *Demokratie in der Kirche* (Limburg, 1970).

the structure of the cosmos the moon is an image for what the Church is in the structure of salvation, in the spiritual-intellectual cosmos. Here primeval symbolism from the history of religion is adopted (although the Fathers did not talk about a "theology of religions", they accomplished it), in which the moon, being a symbol of both fruitfulness and frailty, a symbol of death and transience as well as a symbol of hope and rebirth and resurrection, was an image of human existence, "pathetic and comforting at the same time".[4] Lunar and terrestrial symbolism fuse in many respects. The moon, in both its transience and its rebirth, represents the world of men, the earthly world, the world that is characterized by receiving and neediness, that receives its fruitfulness from somewhere else: from the sun. Thus lunar symbolism simultaneously is a symbol for man, for humanity as represented in woman: receptive and fruitful due to the power of what is received.

The application of the moon symbolism to the Church by the Fathers proceeded mainly from two points of departure: from the connection between moon and woman (mother) and from the idea that the light of the moon is borrowed light, the light of the sun, without which the moon would be mere darkness; it shines, but its light is not its own light but rather the light of another.[5] It is darkness and brightness at the same time. The moon itself

[4] M. Eliade, *Die Religionen und das Heilige* (Salzburg, 1954), 215; see in general the whole chapter in that book entitled "Mond und Mondmystik", 180–216.

[5] See H. Rahner, *Griechische Mythen in christlicher Deutung* (Darmstadt, 1957), 200–224; H. Rahner, *Symbole der Kirche* (Salzburg, 1964), 89–173. He makes the interesting remark that in antiquity natural science thoroughly discussed the question of whether the moon has its own light or some other. Most of the Church Fathers subscribed to the latter theory, which had become the predominant one, and attributed symbolic theological value to it (see esp. p. 100).

is darkness, but it bestows brightness that comes from another heavenly body whose light it transmits. Precisely therein, however, it represents the Church, which shines, even though she herself is dark: she is not bright because of her own light, but, rather, she receives light from the true Sun, Christ, so that she, although only earthly stone herself (like the moon, which, after all, is just another earth), nevertheless can give light in the night of our remoteness from God—"the moon tells of the mystery of Christ."[6]

We should not force symbols; they are valuable precisely because of their figurative nature, which eludes logical schematization. Nevertheless, in the age of moon voyages an expansion of the comparison suggests itself, in which the specific features of our situation (including the reality that is the Church) can be made visible through this contrast of physical and symbolic thought. The moon voyager or moon probe discovers that the moon is only stone, desert, sand, mountains, but not light. And, in fact, in and of itself, it is nothing more: only desert, sand, stone. And yet it is also light—not in itself, but from another source and to another purpose—and it remains so even in the age of space travel. It is what it itself is not. The other thing that is not its own is still its reality, too—as "not its own". There is a truth of physics and there is a truth of poetry, of symbols, and neither cancels the other out. And now I ask: Is that not a very exact image of the Church? Someone who drives over it and extracts samples with a moon probe can discover only desert, sand, and stone, the all-too-human foibles of man and his history with its deserts, its dust, and its heights. That is hers. And yet it is not the essential thing about her. The decisive thing is that she, although only sand and stone

[6] Ambrose, *Exameron* IV, 8, 23; CSEL 32, 1, p. 137, ll. 27f.; H. Rahner, *Griechische Mythen*, 201.

herself, is still light that comes from the Lord, from the other: what is not hers is what is truly and properly hers; indeed, her nature lies in the fact that she herself does not count, but, rather, what counts about her is what she is not, that she exists only in order to be dispossessed—that she has a light that she is not and solely on account of which she nevertheless is. She is "moon"—*mysterium lunae*—and thus she concerns those who believe, for in this very way she is the locus of an abiding spiritual decision.

The state of affairs that I have touched on in this image seems to me to be decisive, and so I would like to clarify it by means of another observation before I try to translate it from the language of imagery into objective statements. After the Mass was translated into German, before the recent [post-conciliar] reform, again and again I ran into a linguistic inhibition that arose from the very same context and symptomatically illustrates once more precisely what we have been talking about. The Latin prayer *Suscipiat*, as prayed in German, asks that the Lord might accept the sacrifice "zum Segen für uns und *Seine* ganze heilige Kirche" (as a blessing for us and for all *his* holy Church). Again and again I found myself saying, "and for all *our* holy Church". This linguistic inhibition makes quite plain the problem we are talking about, and the whole transference we have experienced becomes evident therein. Our Church has taken the place of his Church, and thus many churches have appeared, since everyone has his own. The churches have become *our* endeavors, and we are either proud or ashamed of them; many little private properties stand side by side, "our" churches through and through, which we make for ourselves, which belong to us, and which we try to reshape or maintain accordingly. With all this talk about "our church" or "your church", we have lost sight of "his Church". But that is all that matters, and if she no longer exists, then "our" church ought to abdicate as well. Church that is merely ours is a pointless game in a sandbox.

Why I remain in the Church

But with that we have already given the fundamental answer to the question about which I was asked to speak: I am in the Church because I believe that now as ever "his Church" lives behind "our Church", that we cannot change this situation, and that I can stand by him only if I stand by and in his Church. I am in the Church because, despite everything, I believe that she is at the deepest level not our Church but precisely "his".

To put it quite concretely: It is the Church that, despite all the human foibles of the people in her, gives us Jesus Christ, and only through her can we receive him as a living, authoritative reality that summons and endows me here and now. Henri de Lubac formulated this state of affairs as follows: "Do they realize that if they still receive Christ, it is to the Church they owe it? ... Jesus lives for us. But without the visible continuity of the Church, the desert sands would have long since swallowed up, if not perhaps his name and his memory, certainly the influence of his gospel and faith in his divinity.... 'Without the Church, Christ evaporates or is fragmented or cancels himself out.' And without Christ what would man be?"[7] This elementary acknowledgment has to be made at the start: Whatever infidelity there is or may be in the Church, however true it is that she constantly needs to be measured anew by Jesus Christ, still there is ultimately no opposition between Christ and Church. It is through the Church that he remains alive

[7] H. de Lubac, *The Church: Paradox and Mystery*, trans. James R. Dunne (New York: Ecclesia Press, 1969), 6–7; cf. 4ff.

despite the distance of history, that he speaks to us today, is with us today as master and Lord, as our brother who unites us all as brethren. And because the Church, and she alone, gives us Jesus Christ, causes him to be alive and present in the world, gives birth to him again in every age in the faith and prayer of the people, she gives mankind a light, a support, and a standard without which humanity would be unimaginable. Anyone who wants to find the presence of Jesus Christ in humanity cannot find it contrary to the Church but only in her.

With that we have already made the next point. I am in the Church for the same reasons that I am a Christian in the first place. For one cannot believe alone. One can believe only as a fellow believer. Faith is by its very nature a force for unification. Its primordial image is the story of Pentecost, the miracle of understanding among people who by their origins and history are foreign to one another. Faith is ecclesial or it is not faith. Furthermore, just as one cannot believe alone but only as a fellow believer, neither can one believe on the basis of one's own authority and ingenuity, but only when there is an authorization to believe that is not within my power and does not come from me but rather goes before me. A faith of one's own devising is an oxymoron. For a self-made faith would only vouch for and be able to say what I already am and know anyway; it could not go beyond the boundary of my ego. Hence a self-made Church, a congregation that creates itself, that exists by its own graces, is also an oxymoron. Although faith demands communion, it is the sort of communion that has authority and takes the lead, not the sort that is my own creation, the instrument of my own wishes.

The whole matter can also be formulated in terms of a more historical aspect: Either this Jesus was more than a man, so that he had an inherent authority that was more than the product of his own arbitrary will, or he was not. In other words, either an authority proceeded from him that extends and lasts through the ages, or else he left no such authority behind. In the latter case, I have to rely on my own reconstructions, and then he is nothing more than any other great founding figure that one makes present by reflection. But if he is more than that, then he does not depend on my reconstructions; then the authority he left behind is valid even today.

Let us return to the crucial point: being Christian is possible only in Church. Not close by. And let us not hesitate to ask once more, quite soberly, the solemn-sounding question: Where would the world be without Christ? Without a God who speaks and knows man and whom man can therefore know? Nowadays the attempt to construct such a world is carried on with such grim obstinacy that we know very precisely what the answer is: an absurd experiment. An experiment without any standard. However much Christianity may have failed in practice during its history (and it has failed again and again appallingly), the standards of justice and love have nevertheless emanated from the good news preserved in the Church, even against her will, often in spite of her, and yet never without the quiet power of what has been deposited in her.

In other words: I remain in the Church because I view the faith—which can be practiced only in her and ultimately not against her—as a necessity for man, indeed, for the world, which lives on that faith even when it does not share it. For if there is no more God—and a silent God is no God—then there is no longer any truth that is accessible to the world and to man. In a world without truth, however, one cannot keep on living; even if we suppose that we can do without truth, we still feed on the quiet hope that it has not yet really disappeared, just as the light of the sun could remain for a while after the sun came to an end, momentarily disguising the worldwide night that had started.

We could express the same thing again differently from another perspective: I remain in the Church because only the Church's faith saves man. That sounds very traditional, dogmatic, and unreal, but it is meant quite soberly and realistically. In our world of compulsions and frustrations, the longing for salvation has reawakened with hurricane force. The efforts of Freud and C. G. Jung are just attempts to give redemption to the unredeemed. Marcuse, Adorno, and Habermas continue in their own way, from different starting points, to seek and proclaim salvation. In the background stands Marx, and his question, too, is the question of salvation. The more liberated, enlightened, and powerful man becomes, the more the longing for salvation gnaws at him, the less free he finds himself. The common element in the efforts of Marx, Freud, and Marcuse is that they look for salvation by striving for a world that is delivered from suffering, sickness, and need. A world free of dominion, suffering, and injustice has become the great slogan of our generation; the stormy protests of the young are aimed at this promise, and the resentments of the old rage against the fact that it has not yet been fulfilled, that there still is domination, injustice, and suffering. To fight against suffering and injustice in the world is indeed a thoroughly Christian impulse. But the notion that one can produce a world without suffering through social reform, through the abolition of government and the legal order, and the desire to achieve this here and now are symptoms of false doctrine, of a profound misunderstanding of human nature. Inequality of ownership and power, to tell the truth, are not the only causes of suffering in this world. And suffering is not just the burden that man should throw off: anyone who tries to do that must flee into the illusory world of drugs so as to destroy himself in earnest and come into conflict with reality. Only by suffering himself and by becoming free of the tyranny of egotism through suffering does man find himself, his truth, his joy, his happiness. We are led to believe that one can become a human being without conquering oneself, without the patience of renunciation and the toil of overcoming oneself; that there is no need to withstand the hardship of perseverance or to endure patiently the tension between what man ought to be and what he is in fact: this is the very essence of the crisis of the hour. If a man's hardship is taken away and he is led astray into the fool's paradise of his dreams, he loses what is distinctively his: himself. A human being in fact is saved in no other way but through the cross, through acceptance of his own passion and that of the world, which in God's Passion became the site of liberating meaning. Only in that way, in this acceptance, does a human being become free. All offers that promise it at less expense will fail and prove to be deceptive. The hope of Christianity, the prospect of faith is ultimately based quite simply on the fact that it tells the truth. The prospect of faith is the prospect of truth, which can be obscured and trampled upon, but cannot perish.

We come to our final point. A human being always sees only as much as he loves. Certainly, there is also the clear-sightedness of denial and hatred. But they can see only what is suited to them: the negative. They can thereby preserve love from a blindness in which it overlooks its own limitations and risks. But they cannot build up. Without a certain measure of love, one finds nothing. Someone who does not get involved at least for a while in the experiment of faith, in the experiment of becoming affirmatively involved with the Church, who does not take the risk of looking with the eyes of love, only vexes himself. The venture of

love is the prerequisite for faith. If it is ventured, then one
does not have to hide from the dark areas in the Church.
But one discovers that they are not the only thing after all.
One discovers that alongside the Church history of scandals
there is another Church history that has proved to be fruitful throughout the centuries in great figures such as Augustine, Francis of Assisi, the Dominican priest Las Casas, who
fought passionately for the Indians, Vincent de Paul, and
John XXIII. He finds that the Church has brought forth in
history a gleaming path that cannot be ignored. And the
beauty that has sprung up in response to her message and is
still manifest to us today in incomparable works of art
becomes for him a witness to the truth: something that could
express itself in that way cannot be mere darkness. The beauty
of the great cathedrals, the beauty of the music that has
developed within the context of the faith, the dignity of
the Church's liturgy, and in general the reality of the fes-
tival, which one cannot make for oneself but can only
receive,[8] the elaboration of the seasons in the liturgical year,
in which then and now, time and eternity interpenetrate—
all that is in my view no insignificant accident. Beauty is
the radiance of truth, Thomas Aquinas once said, and one
might add that the distortion of the beautiful is the self-
irony of lost truth. The lasting impression that Christianity
was able to make upon history testifies to the faith, to the
truth that stands behind it.

There is another point that I do not want to omit, even
though it seems to lead us into the realm of subjectivity.
Even today, if you keep your eyes open, you can still meet
people who are a living witness to the liberating power of
the Christian faith. And there is nothing wrong with being

---

[8] On this subject, see esp. J. Pieper, *Leisure, the Basis of Culture* (South
Bend, Ind.: St. Augustine's Press, 1998).

and remaining a Christian, too, on account of the people who exemplified Christianity for us and through their lives made it worth believing and loving. After all, it is an illusion when a human being tries to make himself into a sort of transcendental subject in whom only that which is not accidental has any validity. Certainly there is a duty then to reflect on such experiences, to test their reliability, to purify them and comply with them anew. But even then, in this necessary process of making them objective, is it not a respectable proof of Christianity that it has made human beings human by uniting them with God? Is not the most subjective element here at the same time something completely objective for which we do not have to apologize to anyone?

One more remark at the conclusion. When we speak, as we have done here, about the fact one cannot see anything without love, that one must therefore also learn to love the Church in order to recognize her, many people today become uneasy: Is not love the opposite of criticism? And in the final analysis, is not it the subterfuge of the ruling powers that are trying to divert criticism and maintain the status quo for their own benefit? Do we serve mankind by reassuring it and putting a good face on the present situation, or do we serve them by standing up for them constantly against entrenched injustice and oppressive social structures? Those are very far-reaching questions that cannot be examined here in detail. But one thing ought to be clear: Real love is neither static nor uncritical. If there is any possibility at all of changing another human being for the better, then it is only by loving him and by slowly helping him to change from what he is into what he can be. Should it be any different with the Church? Just look at recent history: in the liturgical and theological renewal during the first half of the twentieth century, a real reform developed that brought about positive change; that was possible only because there were watchful individuals who, with the gift of discernment, loved the Church "critically" and were willing to suffer for her. If nothing succeeds any more today, maybe it is because all of us are all too intent on merely proving ourselves right. Staying in a Church that we actually have to make first in order for her to be worth staying in is just not worthwhile; it is self-contradictory. Remaining in the Church because she is worthy of remaining; because she is worth loving and transforming ever anew through love so that she transcends herself and becomes more fully herself—that is the path that the responsibility of faith shows us even today.

Epilogue

Man in the Presence of God:
Faith, Hope, and Love—An Attempt at a
Theological Profile of Benedict XVI

An intellectual on the Chair of Peter?

Benedict XVI has often been described as an intellectual on the Chair of Peter. This, of course, can lead to misunderstandings: one may then too quickly lose sight of important aspects of Joseph Ratzinger's life and thought or too hastily conclude that one has understood him and the demands and concerns of his work. A man and a thinker of Ratzinger's stature cannot be understood by means of simple slogans—however much people try again and again to reduce his life and thought to slogans. For Benedict XVI is more than an intellectual. Knowledge and erudition are not ends in themselves for him, and their scope is not limited to in-depth studies or learned treatises. For Christian faith, according to Ratzinger, is not a kind of knowledge but, rather, trust and joy: "Someone who is glad from the bottom of his heart, who has suffered and has not lost the capacity for joy, cannot be far from the God of the gospel,

Translated by Michael J. Miller.

whose first word at the threshold of the New Covenant is: Rejoice."

Fundamental acts of a life

The essence of a person is perhaps first revealed when we examine, not merely the themes he repeatedly advances, but the undertakings in which he treats certain themes and questions. There are many ways in which one can discuss Ratzinger's main themes: the modern era, relativism with respect to values and truth, the problems of freedom and autonomy, the limitations and possibilities of human reason, the Church, Mary, Christ, and God. Perhaps the most distinctive thing about Benedict XVI is not necessarily these themes, but, rather, the way in which he approaches these themes, how he makes them his *own* themes: namely, from the standpoint of reception and preservation, transmission and reflection, discipleship and giving witness. We can put it even more pointedly: in a kind of discipleship that he always understands as transmission and preservation as well.

Hence, Ratzinger's fundamental question is: How, from what standpoint, can the message of Christianity be correctly received, preserved, and transmitted, and how can one live thus as a disciple of Christ? Starting from this question, starting from the existential and intellectual undertakings in which he seeks to answer this question, Ratzinger treats the numerous questions that he confronts again and again: Who helps us, first and foremost, to live as human beings? How can we be Christians today? What does it mean in the first place to be a Christian? How can we respond to every word spoken to us [*Zuspruch*] by God, who over and over again calls upon us [*uns in Anspruch nimmt*]? Does truth exist, and, if so, what demand does the truth make upon man? How can we, finite and mortal human beings, respond to this infinite claim and comply with it? How can a human being become really free and live in the truth and true joy? Wherein lies the core of the Christian faith?

Ultimately these various, closely interwoven undertakings prove to be moments in one single existential and intellectual undertaking, one single life in the presence of God, as moments of a life that pays attention to the signs of the times, takes them seriously, but does not consider them absolute, since it claims to know about a truth that is in time yet also points beyond time.

Receiving and preserving

Again and again Ratzinger says that Christian faith is not an ideology, not a world view or philosophy. It is in the first place a gift, a present, and therefore something that was given to us, something that we have received and have to preserve. For we ourselves did not make the faith and its contents, and we cannot arbitrarily change it any way we like, but rather as human beings we must make room in our lives and thoughts for the truth of the faith. But what is essential to this faith? In his volume *Principles of Catholic Theology*, Ratzinger concisely summarized the center of the Christian faith: "confession of the triune God in the *communion* of the Church, in whose solemn remembrance the center of salvation history—the death and Resurrection of the Lord—is truly present". Ratzinger's theological emphases, too, can be understood in terms of this center: doctrine about God and Christology, ecclesiology and questions about the liturgy.

It is Ratzinger's conviction, nevertheless, that this reception and preservation of the faith is becoming more and more difficult these days. The Christian faith today faces numerous challenges that—to put it succinctly—could be described as the challenges of modernity. The fundamental coordinates of modern thought make it increasingly difficult to articulate the claim of Christianity or to understand it in the first place. Unless he is willing to be untrue to himself, the Christian cannot simply become modern and get rid of what appears to be old and passé. But the Christian must not retreat into the ghetto of an idealized past, either, and cherish traditions for their own sake. He must also seek dialogue with the times and address the challenges of modernity. This means also recognizing that modernity is a complex phenomenon, that it has its good side and its rather problematic sides, that there is no *monolithic* modernity. And this caution, a judicious testing, also defines Ratzinger's confrontation with modernity and his attempt to rethink the faith again and again and to preserve it.

Let us take as an example of this the question about relativism or man's freedom. Ratzinger's thought, as commentators have often noted, is without a doubt directed against relativism—but not against every variety of relativism. He opposes a one-sided view that considers relativism to be an absolute as well as the kind of freedom that is no longer capable of acknowledging any unconditional claim. However, Ratzinger certainly does side with the modern separation of theology from politics, or Church from State, and is able to appreciate the findings of the modern philosophy of freedom. In his opinion, Vatican II rightly spoke about an autonomy of earthly matters. The Church rightly should not interfere in all sorts of political questions and must remain critical of attempts to theologize the political realm again—for instance, in liberation theology. And hence there is a right to relativism and human freedom, albeit a right that, in Ratzinger's opinion, is ultimately relative.

On the other hand, there are also questions about which the Church must speak up and point out that man is subject to an unconditional claim, that a relativism set up as an absolute becomes totalitarian and inhumane, that an unrestricted freedom leads to the loss of freedom: for example, when human rights are violated and people no longer heed the foundational truth about who man really is. If, for instance, democracy is exposed to intrinsic dangers, then the word of the Church certainly does have a political dimension as well. For then—Ratzinger repeatedly says in his writings—it is the duty of the Church and of the Christian to recall the order of creation and its truth, to remind man of God and his claim, and to make sure that these considerations have a hearing even in an increasingly secularized public forum. If man wants to live in a human manner, Ratzinger says, he must not do away with the idea of God; he must preserve it, the revelation of God and faith in God. Only then, in the sight of God, can he really live as a human being.

Transmitting and reflecting

When we say that the Christian should understand his faith and make sure that it receives a hearing, this already manifests the other fundamental undertaking: transmission and reflection. Christian theology, for Ratzinger, is always an act of transmitting: in its confrontation with the local culture, in its thoughtful account of our faith and our hope, and in its presentation of that center from which Christian life and thought receive their orientation: Jesus Christ. And so Ratzinger's concern can be understood as concern about a transmission: a transmission, of course, that remains conscious of the fact that there is something to transmit and that the transmission is ultimately a means to an end and not an end in itself. Transmitting is in the service of the truth and is, as Ratzinger says, a task: one that is directed inward but also

outward in ecumenical discussion and in the dialogue with
other religions, world views, and philosophies.

In this attitude of transmitting and reflecting, however,
something else is expressed as well: the fact that this possibility of transmitting exists, that it is possible to build a bridge
between the Church and the world or between Christianity
and modernity. The instrument that makes it possible to build
this bridge is reason. For man, Ratzinger says, is not only
reasonable; his reason is also capable of the truth and ori-
ented to the truth. And, conversely, Christianity in his view
is not contrary to reason but, rather, presupposes reason and
is suprarational. Thus, Christianity for Benedict XVI is the
synthesis of faith and reason. Christianity itself has the character of transmission. And whenever faith and reason are
taken as absolutes and no longer stand in relation to one
another—so Ratzinger has warned us repeatedly and often
urgently—man loses an equilibrium that causes him to live
in a human manner, often with dangerous consequences.

For Ratzinger, however, transmitting is never a purely
theoretical or scholarly matter. It ultimately means giving
witness and also listening to the existential witness of others. Therefore, Ratzinger repeatedly summons us to consider within theology the "theology of the saints" as well,
which is a theology based on experience. For "all real progress
in theological knowledge has its origin in the eye of love
and its faculty of sight."

Discipleship and giving witness

Receiving, preserving, and transmitting the Christian faith
must, therefore, according to Ratzinger, always have a practical dimension as well. It must ultimately come true and
give testimony in everyday life: in energetic action and in
prayerful worship of God, in love of neighbor and love of

God. Without this existential dimension, every theology, all talk about God, would finally be mute. All understanding, for Ratzinger, is based on a standing in the presence of God. This standing before God, however, is not something static. It means following a way, allowing oneself to be touched by God, witnessing to him: "Christian faith is being touched by God and witnessing to him."

This witness finds its most important expression not only in deeds of unselfish love of neighbor, but also in the Church's liturgy. For here, in the liturgy, a space for God is opened up. In its beauty an attempt is made to give honor to the truth, which, for the Christian, as Ratzinger says, is not an abstract principle; rather, it has a face.

And just as the liturgy cannot be the object of our making and planning, so too it must not be subordinated to purposes and goals other than divine worship—not even to such honorable aims as missionary work or catechesis. Hence, Ratzinger often insists also that the mystical component of Christianity should regain its former strength and that we should turn again more decisively to the mystery of God so as to be able to live by this mystery, the encounter with God, and to be his disciples.

Hence, Ratzinger's thought is profoundly theocentric and attempts to reflect on God's action in history. Philosophy and theology for him are not ends in themselves but, rather, are ordered to something quite simple that is already evident in an exemplary fashion in the lives of the saints: a radical orientation toward God and the fullness of time. This theocentric perspective at first glance restricts man and his claims. A second, deeper look, Ratzinger says, reveals that this perspective liberates man to be authentically, happily human. And, similarly, Ratzinger's reminder about the origin and source of Christian theology should liberate theology: from the danger of taking itself too seriously, of following the latest trend, and of failing to see that faith begins with hearing, with listening to a Word that is perpetually addressed to us.

Perhaps that is why Benedict XVI has announced no explicit program for his pontificate, because the Christian ultimately cannot set for himself a program, a "fore-word" (for that is what "program" means originally) that orients and guides his action, but is instead perpetually subject to the demands of a Word. As Benedict XVI showed also in his first encyclical, *Deus Caritas est*, the Christian is perpetually addressed by God (who is love) and called to faith, hope, and love. Therefore, the life of the Christian is, as Ratzinger sees it, always an afterword, an answer, and a correspondence. Hence he is fond of citing John 7:16: "My teaching is not mine...." What teaching he is talking about, what aspects this teaching has, and what this means for the lives of Christians is shown by the various texts in this volume—texts that make the Christian Creed accessible to our contemporaries and that, precisely for that reason, are insightful—and always exciting as well.

Holger Zaborowski (Washington, D.C., and Freiburg im Breisgau)

Sources

What It Means to Be a Christian: Over Everything: Love
In Joseph Ratzinger, *What It Means to Be a Christian.* Translated by Henry Taylor. San Francisco: Ignatius Press, 2006. 65–86.

God: "I Believe in One God, the Father Almighty"
In Joseph Ratzinger, *Principles of Catholic Theology.* Translated by Mary Frances McCarthy, S.N.D. San Francisco: Ignatius Press, 1987. 67–75.

Creation: Belief in Creation and the Theory of Evolution
In Joseph Ratzinger, *Dogma und Verkündigung.* Munich and Freiburg: Erich Wewel Verlag, 1973. 133–36.

Jesus: The Only Begotten Son of God
In Joseph Ratzinger, *Dogma and Preaching.* Translated by Matthew J. O'Connell. Chicago: Franciscan Herald Press, 1985. 3–6.

Incarnate of the Virgin Mary: "You Are Full of Grace"
In Joseph Ratzinger, *Mary: The Church at the Source.* Translated by Adrian Walker. San Francisco: Ignatius Press, 2005. 61–79.

He Was Crucified, Suffered Death, and Was Buried: Good Friday
In Joseph Ratzinger, *Dogma and Preaching.* Translated by Matthew J. O'Connell. Chicago: Franciscan Herald Press, 1985. 32–41.

Descent into Hell—Ascension—Resurrection of the Body: Difficulties with the Apostles' Creed
In Joseph Ratzinger, *Introduction to Christianity*. Translated by J. R. Foster. Revised edition. San Francisco: Ignatius Press, 2004. 293–301, 310–14, 347–56.

Christ the Liberator: "Seek the Things That Are Above" (Colossians 3:1)
In Joseph Ratzinger, *Seek That Which Is Above*. Translated by Graham Harrison. San Francisco: Ignatius Press, 1986. 45–61.

To Judge the Living and the Dead: He Will Come Again
In Joseph Ratzinger, *Introduction to Christianity*. Translated by J. R. Foster. Revised edition. San Francisco: Ignatius Press, 2004. 318–27.

The Holy Spirit: Mind, Spirit, and Love
In Joseph Ratzinger, *Dogma and Preaching*. Translated by Matthew J. O'Connell. Chicago: Franciscan Herald Press, 1985. 66–71.

One, Holy, Catholic, and Apostolic Church: Church as the Locus of Service to the Faith
In Joseph Ratzinger, *Dogma und Verkündigung*. Munich and Freiburg: Erich Wewel Verlag, 1973. 255.

The Communion of Saints: What Do the Saints Really Mean for Us?
In Franz Breid, ed., *Buße—Umkehr: Formen der Vergebung*. Steyr: W. Ennsthaler Verlag, 1992. 250–56.

The Forgiveness of Sins: Metanoia as the Fundamental Datum of Christian Existence
In Ernst C. Suttner, ed., *Buße und Beichte: Drittes Regensburger Ökumenisches Symposion*. Regensburg: Verlag

Friedrich Pustet, 1972. 21–37. © Libreria Editrice Vaticana, Vatican City.

Resurrection of the Dead and the Life of the World to Come: Beyond Death
In *Communio*, vol. 1, no. 3 (1972): 157–65.

The Church's Credo: Why I Am Still in the Church
In Hans Urs von Balthasar and Joseph Ratzinger, *Zwei Plädoyers*. Munich: Kösel-Verlag, 1971. 57–75.